Leisure, Pleasure – and Duty

The daily life of Silahdar Mustafa, éminence grise in the final years of Murad IV (1635–1640)

Otto Spies Memorial Lecture

edd. Stephan Conermann & Gül Şen

Volume 2

Hedda Reindl-Kiel

Leisure, Pleasure – and Duty

The daily life of Silahdar Mustafa, éminence grise in the final years of Murad IV (1635–1640)

ebv
BERLIN

EBVERLAG

Bibliographic information published by Deutsche Nationalbibliothek
Die Deutsche Nationalbibliothek lists this publication in the Deutsche Nationalbibliografie; detailed bibliographic data are available at [http://dnb.ddb.de].

Images on the cover: *top*: Aqueduct of Mustafa Pasha, (late 1490s), near Skopje
Photo © Machiel Kiel, 2005.
below: Entrance to the "Institut für Orient- und Asienwissenschaften" formerly called Orientalisches Seminar, Bonn
Photo © Gül Şen, 2015.

Layout: Rainer Kuhl

ISBN: 978-3-86893-215-7

Homepage: www.ebverlag.de
E-Mail: post@ebverlag.de

Printed in Germany

Leisure, Pleasure – and Duty
The daily life of Silahdar Mustafa, éminence grise in the final years of Murad IV (1635–1640)[1]

Hedda Reindl-Kiel

Silahdar Mustafa Pasha, the hero of this paper, would have been utterly stunned by its title. Particularly the division between 'leisure' and 'pleasure' would have amazed him, as the Ottoman Turkish of his time did not have a precise and unambiguous word for 'leisure' separated from 'pleasure'. A proper word for leisure was also lacking in the pasha's native South Slavic 'Bosnian'.[2] Moreover, the notion of time split into fixed hours of duty (work) and hours of self-determined activity (or rest) might not yet have entered Ottoman minds.

Peter Burke has demonstrated that in Europe the concept of leisure (especially among the elite) started to develop from Renaissance times, but only really took off as a broader, popular phenomenon in the 18th century, which does not imply, however, that people had not been enjoying merrymaking or *dolce far niente* before.[3] In an interesting article

---

1 The research for this article was largely done during my stay as a Senior Fellow at the Research Center for Anatolian Civilizations of Koç University in 2013/14. I would like to express my gratitude for this wonderful opportunity, the financial support and the assistance I received from all staff members.

2 Nenad Moačanin has kindly informed me that he was not able to find a precise equivalent for the Latin *otium* (leisure) in Bosnian/Croatian/Serbian of the 17th century, only *praznik* (holiday) and *dokolica* derived from *dokon* (idle). Bosnian also contains Turcisms: *uzur* (from *huzur*, 'peace of mind') and almost in the same sense *rahatluk*. I thank him very much for this valuable piece of information.

3 Peter Burke, "The Invention of Leisure in Early Modern Europe", *Past & Present* 146 (1995), pp. 136–150. Joan-Lluís Marfany, "Debate: The Invention of Leisure in Early Modern Europe", *Past & Present* 156 (1997), pp. 174–191; Peter Burke, "Reply", ibidem, pp. 192–197, esp. p. 196. For a good summary of these articles see Marinos Sariyannis, "Time, Work and Pleasure: A Preliminary Approach to Leisure in Ottoman Mentality", idem (ed.), New Trends in Ottoman Studies: Papers presented at the 20th CIÉPO Symposium, Rethymno, 27 June – 1 July 2012, pp. 797–811, esp. 798–799. E-publication: http://www.univie.ac.at/ciepo/wordpress/wp-content/uploads/2011/07/downloaded1.pdf

Cemal Kafadar has linked the urban population's increasing use of night-time for socialising, amusement, labour and new forms of entertainment with the spread of coffee and coffeehouses.[4] In this context he explored the changing meanings of Turkish/Ottoman *eğlenmek*, which in modern language means 'to amuse oneself, to have a good time'. Surprisingly, the oldest denotation (from the 14th to the 18th century) was 'to stop and rest, to spend some time (someplace).' But by the 17th century the term had acquired an additional meaning, and Evliya Çelebi uses it more or less in the same sense the word has today.[5] Meninski's dictionary from 1680 has 'stay, pastime, diversion, and delay'.[6] Thus, albeit still on slippery ground for the thirties of the 17th century, we might say, *eğlence,* would denote 'pleasure, amusement' and also something pretty close to 'leisure'.

It might well be that the new understanding of the word was, in the early 17th century, still only common in elite parlance. We must not forget that Evliya belonged *qua* birth and education to the urbanite upper echelons of society. In his Book of Travels he perceived and described people who were mainly his socially equals or of higher rank. For him the lower classes of society, such as the rural population or urban petty bourgeois, were virtually out of focus.

As Silahdar Mustafa Pasha, the hero of this tale, might be seen as an embodiment of privileged life and elitism, the question of whether leisure and pleasure for an ordinary Ottoman of the first half of the 17th

(accessed 12 October 2015) This stimulating article constitutes a first endeavour to study the Ottoman approach to leisure.

4 Cemal Kafadar, "How Dark is the History of the Night, How Black the Story of Coffee, How Bitter the Tale of Love: The Changing Measure of Leisure and Pleasure in Early Modern Istanbul", Arzu Öztürkmen and Evelyn Birge Vitz (eds.), *Medieval and Early Modern Performance in the Eastern Mediterranean.* Turnhout: Brepols, 2014, pp. 243–269.

5 Kafadar, "How Dark is the History of the Night", p. 249.

6 Franciscus à Mesgnien Meninski, *Thesaurus Linguarum Orientalium Turcicae, Arabicae, Persicae: Praecipuas earum opes a Turcis peculiariter usurpatas continens nimirum lexicon Turcico-Arabico-Persicum ....& grammaticam Turcicam... etc.* Viennae 1680, col. 357 (Latin, German, Italian and French: '*Occupatio, oblectamentum & mora. Verweilung/ Zeitvertreibung/ Kurzweil/ und Verzug. Occupatione, trattimento, passatempo & Indugio, dimora, tardanza. Entretien, occupation, passetemps & retardement.*')

century were one single notion is probably of secondary importance. As our perspective on the pasha, his pleasures, duties and his everyday life is primarily shaped by account books, we should commence our narrative with a short glance to our sources.

The sources and their peculiarities

We rely predominantly on two rather long large-format treasury registers covering the years 1635–40.[7] Both documents are clearly related, with the second record evidently being an extension of the first. Typically for treasury inventories, their organising principle is only partially chronological; the nature of incoming or outgoing items had priority when drawing up such a document. Unlike the treasury registers of other grandees, they record not only objects purchased or received as gifts but also cash coming in and the details of how this money was spent.[8] Many purses full of cash came in as gifts, which is by no means unusual in the 16th and 17th centuries and not automatically connected with corruption. We cannot, however, tell whether some of the purses were meant as bribes. It is difficult to calculate the monetary value, as next to *guruş* (from Ital. *grosso*, via German *Groschen*; large silver coin) three kinds of *akçe* (small silver coin) were involved.

Since a lot of this money was used up in paying tips, the books give us an opportunity to trace aspects of the pasha's everyday life, especially thanks to entries in the second register. A considerable amount of money was spent on charity and alms; support was provided most notably to the weak and the ill,[9] while the young pages, i.e. *oğlancık* ("little

7 Topkapı Sarayı Müzesi Arşivi (henceforth: TSMA), D. 525 (Muharrem 1045 H/July 1635-Şa'ban 1648 H/end of December 1638), 89 folios. D. 2014 (Muharrem 1049 H/ May 1639–Zilhicce 1049 H/April 1640), 16 folios.

8 TSMA, D. 9575 is another inventory, which clearly was owned by Silahdar Mustafa Pasha. It lists only the gifts received during outings. These gifts are, however, also recorded in D. 2014.

9 A good example is his payment of 13,000 *akçe* to a certain Hüseyin, which was a quarter of the man's debts, for which he had been jailed; TSMA, D. 3194, fol. 34b (on the register v. i.). In the autumn of 1636 200 *akçe* were spent on fruits "for the ill"

boys"), were particularly pampered. From time to time the pasha would organise a *yağma*, a "plundering" of coins for his servants, foremost his pages.[10] In the royal palace the *yağma* was an integral part of important feasts;[11] it would be arranged with food offerings, mostly sweetmeats. Bowls filled with delicacies would be placed on the floor and, at a sign from their commander, the janissaries would storm forth and "plunder" the dishes. In the courtly ceremonial coins would also be scattered by chamberlains (in the name of the sultan of course) on occasions such as the discharge of pages who had completed their training.[12] Silahdar Mustafa, too, would take the royal pages into consideration and supply them with pocket money.[13]

In the cash version of *yağma* our pasha himself would throw the coins onto the ground[14] in a ceremony that might not have been any different from the custom in the royal palace. It is all these details, which reveal quite something about the pasha's personality, that make the records extremely charming.

The registers apparently represent only the book-keeping for matters outside the pasha's palace, as they do not cover daily expenses for food and other necessities of life or wages. Several entries indicate the existence of other registers,[15] mentioning at one point a 'great' *defter.*[16] This might be identical with "Mehmed Efendi's register", which is referred to a number of times.[17] The archives of the Topkapı Sarayı contain a

(*hastalara*); ibidem, fol. 37a. On 12 June 1637 Silahdar Mustafa spent 4,000 *akçe* to have food cooked for the ill in the Süleymaniye hospital (*timarhane*): a refined dish of rice (*dane*) and of a sweet rice pudding with saffron (*zerde*); ibidem, fol. 40a.

10 D. 525, fols. 4a, 66a, 70b. D. 2014, fol. 4b.

11 See Hedda Reindl-Kiel, "The Chickens of Paradise: Official Meals in the Mid-Seventeenth Century Ottoman Palace", Suraiya Faroqhi & Christoph K. Neumann (eds.), *The Illuminated Table, the Prosperous House: Food and Shelter in Ottoman Material Culture.* Würzburg: Ergon Verlag, 2003, pp. 67–69.

12 See Gülru Necipoğlu, *Architecture, Ceremonial, And Power: The Topkapı Palace in the fifteenth and sixteenth centuries.* New York: Architectural History Foundation; Cambridge, Mass. – London: The MIT Press, 1991, pp. 117–118.

13 D. 525, fol. 4a, 11b.

14 D. 2014, fol. 4b.

15 D. 525, fols. 6a, 8b, 10b, 12b, 13a. D. 2014, fol. 15b.

16 D. 525, fol. 6a. This entry is, however, made on the march to Baghdad.

17 D. 525, fols. 17b, 20b, 22b, 32b. D. 2014, fol. 15b.

lengthy bookkeeping-cum-treasury register of Silahdar Mustafa Pasha.[18] The scope of this record suggests that it is identical with the 'great' *defter*, but to gain certainty a future detailed study of all registers would be indispensable. Therefore we will refer to it as the 'long' register and to the *defters* mentioned above as 'brief' registers. As for buildings or other major expenses, separate records were kept,[19] but, contrary to our expectations, for the greater part they were not copied into the 'long' *defter*.[20]

Both 'brief' inventories have one great shortcoming: they do not disclose the name of their original owner, who appears only as *sahib-i devlet* (lit. "possessor of luck; lucky fellow"). It is generally thought[21] that the term pointed to the grand vizier. Only after producing a profile of the movements of the register's original owner was I able to rule out the most obvious candidate, Tabanıyassı Mehmed Pasha, then the incumbent grand vizier and not a particular friend of Silahdar Mustafa.[22]

The contents of the two 'brief' records suggest a very close relationship between the owner and Murad IV. The official sometimes made very valuable presents to his lord, such as sable furs at the Feast of Sacrifice in 1638 and, shortly after at the outset of the Baghdad campaign,[23] as a whole collection of jewelled vessels in summer and autumn of 1639.[24] On 10 September 1636 the pasha had acquired emerald buttons (for

18 TSMA, D. 3194; 142 folios.

19 D. 525, fols. 15a, 66a, 72a. D. 2014, fol. 3a.

20 Only smaller constructions or alterations appear in this register, such as the installation of water pipes (10,072 *akçe*) combined with a renovation of the *hamam* in the Pasha's palace (D. 3194, fol. 102b) or the building of the upper structure of a well (*kuyu*) in Üsküdar (ibidem, fol. 103a).

21 Cf. Mehmet Zeki Pakalın, *Osmanlı Tarih Deyimleri ve Terimleri Sözlüğü*. III. [2]Istanbul: Millî Eğitim Basımevi, 1971, p. 93.

22 Naima depicts Silahdar Mustafa even as the *spiritus rector* of Tabanıyassı's execution; Naîmâ Mustafa Efendi, *Târih-i Na'îmâ (Ravzatü 'l-Hüseyn fî Hulâsati Ahbâri 'l-Hâfikayn)*. Mehmet İpşirli (ed.), Ankara: TKK, 2007 (henceforth: *Târih-i Na'îmâ*), vol. II, pp. 922–926. Nejat Göyünç, "Eski Malatya'da Silâhdar Mustafa Paşa Hanı", *İstanbul Üniversitesi Edebiyat Fakültesi Tarih Enstitüsü Dergisi* I (1970), p. 77.

23 D. 525, fol. 87a.

24 D. 2014, fol. 10a. In this time (8 September 1639) he gave a pearl-studded fan, a gift from his own major-domo Hüseyin, as a present to the sultan; ibidem, fol. 10b.

14,400 *akçe*) for the sultan's cloak (*kerrake*) of cashmere shawl.[25] The present of a golden longneck bottle (440 *dirhem*/1,411 g), costing the lordly sum of 99,160 *akçe,* was intended to make the Feast of Sacrifice in 1637 pleasant for Murad IV.[26] A jewelled crystal goblet (*kupa*), worth 37,000 *akçe,* was probably destined for the sultan on the Day of Ashura.[27]

An inventory of gifts to the sultan, ending up in the treasury of the royal stables, lists a lavish present of precious horse tacks and trappings Silahdar Mustafa offered his lord on 26 July 1639.[28] Without any doubt this accoutrement was carried to the royal palace on matching noble horses which were included in the gift, but listed in a different record.

Yet the registers also refer several times to unpretentious garments tailored for the sultan, for example on 20 Ramazan 1046 (5 February 1637) a *cübbe-don* of *kutni* for the *Şeker Bayramı* (Sugar Feast; in the document wrongly labelled as *büyük bayram,* "the great holiday", which denotes the Feast of Sacrifice).[29] *Cübbe-don* stands here for a full set of outer garments, i.e. *don* is not used as underpants but as a dress, while *cübbe* resembles a robe or a sur-kaftan.[30]

Presenting the sultan with garments might not have been entirely outlandish, but having bespoke clothes tailored for him points to a fairly intimate friendship.[31] This is also corroborated by an entry indicating that Silahdar Mustafa's treasurer had paid (by order of the pasha) 4 *guruş* for the rent of the boat bringing the sultan to the Topkapı Palace for giving audience (*'arz*) on 30 June 1639.[32]

It even seems that the official owning the register was partly living at the royal court. Entries such as *içerüye sahib-i devlet hazretlerine*

25 D. 3194, fol. 36b.
26 D. 3194, fol. 39b.
27 D. 3194, fol. 40a.
28 TSMA, D. 10034, fol. 1b.
29 D. 525, fol. 3b.
30 Cf. Reşad Ekrem Koçu, *Türk Giyim, Kuşam ve Süslenme Sözlüğü.* Ankara: Sümerbank, 1967, pp. 57–58.
31 D. 3194, fol 18a, mentions two kaftans of the sultan, which served as models (*nümune*) for fashioning new clothes.
32 D. 2014, fol. 2a.

gönderildi[33] ("sent to the inside [of the royal court], to his Excellency the auspicious vizier") hint to such an intimate connection. The 'long' *defter* reveals even that Silahdar Mustafa used the royal treasury to store his valuables.[34] At one point the second 'brief' register refers to the defective door of our vizier's dwelling (*oda*) in Davudpaşa,[35] which must have been situated on the palace grounds there.

Silahdar Mustafa Pasha's career

I was ultimately able to attribute the registers, with a high degree of certainty, to Bazergânzade (or Tüccarzade) Silahdar Mustafa Pasha, who was the second vizier at the time in question but not a major protagonist in the contemporary chronicles.[36] Mustafa Pasha, despite being the most powerful man after the sultan, never made it to the rank of grand vizierate but became second vizier on 23 May 1635 (6 Zilhicce 1044 H),[37] so the term *sahib-i devlet* cannot have been reserved only for the grand vizier but must have been used generally for the rank of vizier.[38]

---

33 D. 525, fol. 2b and passim. In contrast to *içerüye* we find entries such as: *Üsküdar'da sahib-i devlet bin altunı kese[ye] koyub hazinedar ağa saraya götürmüşdür* ("In Üsküdar the auspicious vizier put thousand gold pieces into a purse and the treasurer brought it to the palace"), D. 2014, fol. 10b. From other entries it is evident that this palace was situated in Istanbul proper.

34 D. 3194, fol. 2b (*Sa'adetlü sahib-i devlet Silahdar Paşa – yessere 'llahu muradehu ve ma yeşa - hazretlerinin hazine-i 'amirelerine dahil olan akçe ve sa'ir hedayayı beyan eder*).

35 D. 2014, fol. 3b.

36 Göyünç, "Eski Malatya'da Silâhdar Mustafa Paşa Hanı", pp. 69–83, gives quite a detailed biography of the pasha using chronicles and a great number of archival documents.

37 *Târih-i Na'îmâ* II, p. 803. Peçuyî reports his appointment as second vizier for late spring/early summer 1635 and underscores that the *silahdar* (sword-bearer) was Murad IV's boon companion (*nedim*). Thus, Mustafa Pasha would continue to serve his lord in his private quarters and be around him day and night; Peçevî İbrahim Efendi, *Tarîh-i Peçevî*. Fahri Ç. Derin and Vahit Çabuk (eds.), Istanbul: Enderun Kitabevi, 1980, p. 431.

38 The earliest date given in Mustafa Pasha's first 'brief' register (D. 525, fol. 87b) is 20 Muharrem 1045 H (6 July 1635). In this context he is mentioned as *sahib-i devlet*. Another example for this use are Başbakanlık Osmanlı Arşivi, MAD 6067 and MAD 14724, dealing with the governor-general of Aleppo in the rank of vizier (1658–59 and

The Kaiser's envoy, Schmid vom Schwarzenhorn describes "Silichtar Bassa" as extremely rich and very much in favour with the queen mother (*valide sultan*),[39] Kösem Mahpeyker. A Venetian contemporary witness (quoted by Hammer) states that Mustafa was born in Sarajevo as son of a Turkish merchant trading with Venice and that he was only 26 years old on his appointment as second vizier.[40]

According to Naima, Mustafa was the third son of Haccı Sinan ed-Din Yusuf, a wealthy merchant of Sarajevo.[41] The prosperous family background is also indicated by a dervish convent (the "Hadži- Sinanova Tekija") which Mustafa's father erected in Sarajevo, by the *türbe* (mausoleum) of Haccı Sinan, and the elaborate gravestone of Mustafa's mother Sakine Hatun (died in 1618/19).[42] Her early death might have been the reason why his father put him (and possibly his brother Mehmed[43]) into the service of a high-ranking official.

1665), in all probability Kethüda Gürcü Mehmed Pasha, who is non-identical with the former grand vizier Gürcü Mehmed Pasha.

39 Johann Rudolf Schmid zum Schwarzenhorn, "Finalrelation Nr. 1", ed. Peter Meienberger, *Johann Rudolf Schmid zum Schwarzenhorn als kaiserlicher Resident in Konstantinopel in den Jahren 1629–1643*, p. 165.

40 Joseph von Hammer, *Geschichte des osmanischen Reiches*. (Henceforth: *GOR*) V, Pest 1829, reprint: Graz: Akademische Druck- u. Verlagsanstalt, 1965, p. 681.

41 *Târih-i Na'îmâ* II, p. 789. The 'long' register refers, for April 1636 to the pasha's younger brother Mahmud as receiving a gift of 100,000 *akçe*; D. 3194, fol. 34b; he appears, without mentioning his name, as donor of a sword inlaid with gold; ibidem, fol. 76a. He surfaces two times more, once as a donor and once as recipient of a tent with mosquito net (*namusiye*), ibidem, fols. 17a, 103b. Another brother (*birader*) named Mehmed Ağa appears several times; ibidem, fols. 6a, 6b, 17a, 57a. A certain İbrahim Çelebi, labelled a relative (*akraba*) of the pasha, received on 25 October 1636 a gift of 20,000 *akçe*, ibidem, fol. 37a.

42 Mehmed Mujezinović, *Islamska Epigrafika u Bosni i Hercegovini*. I. Sarajevo: Veselin Masleša, 1974, pp. 247–256, 232, 233.

43 He is referred to as "giving" (*verdüği*) a scimitar (*çintiyan*), while his brother Mahmud "sent" (*gönderdüği*) the blade of a 'Frankish' sword; D. 3194, fol. 17a. At an unknown date (probably 1636–7) the pasha provided the basic furnishings of Mehmed's house (felts for the floor, cushions, sitting pads and cupboards for storing cushions and beddings); ibidem, fol. 57a. This might have been the time when Mehmed had finished his training in the official's household or the royal palace and set up his own household. On 13 October 1637 the pasha gave Mehmed 50,000 *akçe* in order that the money be used for alms by their father in Bosnia; ibidem, fol. 40b.

Naima links the final downfall of Abaza Pasha with Silahdar Mustafa's secret agitation against him. Naima says that Abaza, while serving as governor-general of Bosnia, had moved against Haccı Sinan, whose assets he wanted to seize. According to this account, Abaza imprisoned the merchant and threatened him with death, but the old man remained steadfast.[44] This story again suggests that the family belonged to the urban patrician class of Sarajevo.

Mustafa started his career in the service of several grandees (*ekabir*), such as Hattât Hasan Pasha,[45] obviously a native of Sarajevo himself,[46] a former page (*iç oğlanı*) of the royal palace,[47] then, in 1632, general of the janissaries (*yeniçeri ağası*) and, in 1633, governor-general of Bosnia.[48] In all likelihood Mustafa's incorporation into the household of Hattât Hasan Pasha was arranged through connections of Haccı Sinan. For some reason, Naima continues, young Mustafa withdrew from this service and entered the corps of the royal pages (*gılman-ı hassa*). More likely than not, however, this transfer was secured by Hattat Hasan Pasha before he set out for Bosnia.

Furthermore, Naima relates that Mustafa attracted the attention of the sultan, who incorporated him into his *hass oda* (privy chamber) having been charmed by his brave horsemanship and enthusiasm for ceremonious behaviour.[49] Murad VI's affection for and benevolence towards him was, claims Naima, a hundred times stronger than the monarch's earlier inclination towards his late and much lamented favourite Musa (who had been murdered during an uprising in 1632). Mustafa, for his part, was said to have served his lord with unique devotion and complete sincerity. The sultan would not have him leave his side for a single moment as Mustafa became an éminence grise whose voice was

44 *Târih-i Na'îmâ* II, p. 793.
45 *Târih-i Na'îmâ* II, p. 789.
46 *Târih-i Na'îmâ* II, p. 790.
47 İsmail Hakkı Uzunçarşılı, *Osmanlı Devletinin Saray Teşkilâtı.* ^{2}Ankara: TTK, 1984, p. 335.
48 *Târih-i Na'îmâ* II, p. 709 and 760.
49 His adherence to the rules of protocol is even palpable in his bookkeeping, where it says: "according to the protocol book, bonus payment [for the Feast of Sacrifice] to the officials of the *divan* chancery (*ehl-i divan*): 2,930 [*akçe*]", D. 3194, fol. 34b.

increasingly heard. This influence enabled him, for instance, to save the life of many men the ruler had destined for execution.[50]

Paul Rycaut reports that Murad IV had selected him "for his beauty only" from the boys educated at Galatasaray and made him a page of his *hass oda* and after a short time his sword bearer (*silahdar ağa*).[51] Mustafa might indeed have been trained at Galatasaray; once (probably for the Sacrifice Feast in 1638) he bought lambs for the pages of this institution, which suggests a possible affiliation.

According to Naima, Mustafa, who was already a courtier (*mukarreb*) of the sultan, became *silahdar* in 1634,[52] in 1635 second vizier, and shortly afterwards (end of Zilhicce 1044/mid-June 1635) governor-general of Syria (Şam).[53] The previous governor of that prestigious province, Küçük Ahmed Pasha, who was now appointed governor-general of Erzurum, seems to have been dissatisfied with the latter position. Hence, the sultan proposed that he should give 20,000 gold pieces to Silahdar Pasha to relinquish, thus making the way for Küçük Ahmed's return to the province. And, according to Naima, this was what Küçük Ahmed did.[54] The timing of this deal is, however, not quite clear. Mustafa Pasha's first register notes for 14 Cemazi I 1046 H/14 October 1636 a sumptuous gift parcel from Şa'ban Efendi, the *kadı* of Damascus.[55] This courtesy suggests that our pasha was still in charge for the province of Syria.

In July 1636 a change in Silahdar Mustafa Pasha's official status might have taken place, since he had a new seal engraved.[56] Küçük Ahmed Pasha must have regained Şam on one day or another in spring

50 *Târih-i Na'îmâ* II, p. 789. For the royal favourite in the late 16th and early 17th centuries see Günhan Börekçi, *Factions and Favorites at the Courts of Sultan Ahmed I (r. 1603–17) and his Immediate Predecessors*. Unpublished PhD thesis, The Ohio State University, 2010.

51 Sir Paul Ricaut, *History of the Present State of the Ottoman Empire*. 3London: R. Clavell, J. Robinson and A. Churchill, 1686, p. 61.

52 *Târih-i Na'îmâ* II, p. 791.

53 *Târih-i Na'îmâ* II, p. 805, 811. Göyünç, "Eski Malatya'da Silâhdar Mustafa Paşa Hanı", p. 70.

54 *Târih-i Na'îmâ* II, p. 805-806. Göyünç, "Eski Malatya'da Silâhdar Mustafa Paşa Hanı", p. 70.

55 D. 525, fol. 3a.

56 D. 525, fols. 70a/b, 82b.

1637, as on 5 April of that year his *mütesellim* (lieutenant-governor), Mehmed Ağa, coming from Damascus, delivered gifts to Mustafa Pasha.[57] But the former *silahdar*'s connection with Syria had not yet ended, since he was re-appointed governor-general of Şam on 5 September 1638.[58] During both terms in this office Silahdar Mustafa seems to have administered the province only nominally. The official duties were conducted on the ground by his *mütesellim* Çifteli (Çiftelerli) 'Osman Agha.[59] Çifteli 'Osman Ağa is mentioned repeatedly in the first 'brief' inventory, albeit without his actual function.[60]

Mustafa Pasha's second tenure in Syria was again short-lived: Directly after the conquest of Baghdad in 1638 he was appointed admiral of the fleet.[61] Yet, after his return from the campaign he did not leave the Ottoman capital for naval expeditions but looked after the administration of the fleet and the building of new ships[62] (v. *infra*). It might not so much have been his lack of nautical experience but the worry about his ill lord and soul mate, which explains this choice.

Good looks

As to be expected, and indicated by Rycaut, Mustafa's handsomeness must have played a role when Murad IV chose him as his favourite companion. Hammer's Venetian source, which must have been penned shortly after Mustafa's appointment as second vizier, describes him as having virile features but still wearing no beard, only a moustache.[63] This

57 D. 525, fol. 10b.

58 Buğra Atsız, *Das Osmanische Reich um die Mitte des 17. Jahrhunderts*. München: Dr. Dr. Trofenik, 1977, p. 4 (Cod. 894 Warn., fol. 6a). Göyünç, "Eski Malatya'da Silâhdar Mustafa Paşa Hanı", p. 71 (erroneously 25 Rebi' I 1048 H is given as 5 August 1638).

59 *Târih-i Na'îmâ* II, p. 823. 'Abdülkādir Efendi, *Topçular Kâtibi 'Abdülkādir (Kadrî) Efendi Tarihi.* (Metin ve Tahlîl) II. Ziya Yılmazer (ed.), Ankara: TTK, 2003, (henceforth: *'Abdülkādir Efendi Tarihi*) p. 1090.

60 D. 525, fols. 6b, 11b, 70a, 83b.

61 *Târih-i Na'îmâ* II, p. 894.

62 Cf. Göyünç, "Eski Malatya'da Silâhdar Mustafa Paşa Hanı", p. 72.

63 Hammer, *GOR* V, p. 681.

would have been due to the rule that no officer (except the *bostancıbaşı*, the 'head gardener') in the service of the sultan was allowed to grow a beard, but only a moustache.[64] Mustafa's barefacedness must have been a reminder of his former status and was soon to change.

Silahdar Mustafa's good looks must have been underscored by his sartorial elegance. To conclude from the plethora of entries referring to garments and their making in the 'long' register, a whole army of tailors and passement makers must have worked for him and his household.[65]

He must have been greatly cherished by Istanbul's merchants of luxury goods, particularly jewellers and gem traders, as he was probably their top customer. He bought, for example, sable fur in an enormous quantity, namely 15 'bales', and disbursed for them 444,000 *akçe*.[66] In May 1636 he had spent the same sum for an unspecified aigrette he bought from the Jew Menachim,[67] which was followed at the begin of the next year by a diamond *sorguç* (aigrette) of the highest quality, accordingly 720,000 *akçe* had to be stumped up.[68] On 27 June 1637 a number of diamonds were purchased (at 6,780 *akçe*) for a jewelled belt – explicitly made for the pasha – and the piece was completed with a range of other diamonds taken from the treasury.[69] This was by no means the only diamond belt he owned: already in January he had lashed out on one 300,000 *akçe*[70] and on 13 October of this year he blew more than half a million of *akçe* for another two of these costly girdles.[71] The glittering

64 [Ignatius] M[ouradgea] d'Ohsson, *Tableau général de l'empire Othoman, divisé en deux parties, dont l'une comprend la Législation Mahométane; l'autre, L'Histoire de l'Empire Othoman*. VI/1, Paris: imprimerie de monsieur [Firmin Didot] 1791, pp. 127–129.

65 D. 3194, fols. 47b–50b, 52a/b, 54a, 59a–62a, 64a–68b, 73a–74a, 77a/b.

66 D. 3194, fol. 41a. The entry does not bear a date, but can be dated probably November 1637.

67 D. 3194, fol. 34b. An unskilled labourer would have had to work more than 81 years for this sum, cf. Şevket Pamuk, *İstanbul ve Diger Kentlerde 500 Yıllık Fiyatlar ve Ücretler, 1469–1998/500 Years of Prices and Wages in Istanbul and Other Cities*. Ankara: T.C. Başbakanlık Devlet İstatistik Enstitüsü, 2000, p. 70.

68 D. 3194, fol. 39a.

69 D. 3194, fol. 40a.

70 D. 3194, fol. 39a.

71 One of them had 204 stones and was purchased from the brother of Yakov for 240,000 *akçe*, the other, with 227 stones, from Yakov at 302,400 *akçe*. Additionally sixteen "naked" (*çıplak*) diamonds were acquired for 57,600 *akçe*; D. 3194, fol. 41a.

stones must have fascinated him very much, as the Jew Arslan sold him 40 diamonds more only a month later.[72] The latter's coreligionist Yakov supplied the pasha with diamond froggings.[73] In December 1637 Silahdar Mustafa acquired 535 diamonds, costing 638,850 *akçe*, from the Jew Yakov to adorn a sword, and a ruby of more than 14 carat (*kırat* 14, *buğday* 1) for 75,600 *akçe*. Around the same time a sapphire (*gök yakut*) for an armband (*pazubend*) was obtained for the relatively modest sum of 9,600 akçe.[74] As sapphires rarely occur in Ottoman jewellery,[75] the latter stone (probably coming from Ceylon; Cashmere sapphires were not yet known) and the many diamonds suggest a highly sophisticated, exclusive taste. After all, in those years diamonds were still a rather uncommon gem in Ottoman luxury adornments, but nevertheless they signalled great wealth and above all political power.

The preference for precious and rare luxury objects is also reflected in Silahdar Mustafa's acquisition of 12 celadon vessels on 8 February 1638 for 28,560 *akçe*.[76] But even this kind of luxury could be surpassed: the Chinese porcelain used on the Feast of Sacrifice was jewelled.[77] The pasha and his guests would not wash their hands with water poured out from an ordinary pitcher and flowing into an ordinary bowl, they would be served with a jewelled set of pitcher and bowl (*leğen – ibrik*) in "Indian style", bought on 6 April 1637 for the amazing sum of 540,000 *akçe*.[78]

The pasha's collection of shoes is remarkable: one entry records the purchase – explicitly for the pasha himself – of 43 pairs of normal shoes

---

72 The stones costed 6 *guruş* (1 *guruş* = 120 *akçe*) per piece, thus 28,800 *akçe* were spent; D. 3194, fol. 41a.

73 Silahdar Mustafa paid for them 102,000 *akçe* on 8 March 1638; D. 3194, fol. 42b.

74 Whether 70,000 *akçe* paid to Yakov on 23 January 1638 for diamond(s) on a sword hilt were the arrearage of the 535 diamonds or for new stones is not clear; D. 3194, fol. 41b. On 10 February Yakov received another 116,400 *akçe* for diamonds destined for the "jewelled sword"; ibidem, fol. 42a.

75 Gül İrepoğlu, *Imperial Ottoman Jewellery: reading history through jewellery*. Feyza Howell (trsl.), Istanbul: BKG, 2012, p. 61, states that the first known example of the use of sapphires comes from the time of Murad IV, followed by four specimens from the middle of the 17th century.

76 D. 3194, fol. 42a.

77 D. 3194, fol. 40a.

78 D. 3194, fol. 39b.

(*pabuç*), of 84 pairs of soft leather socks worn inside shoes (*mest*), 32 pairs of boots (*çizme*), 40 pairs of *Çerkesî* shoes and 77 pairs of indoor slippers.[79] All these luxury acquisitions suggest a life in great style and maybe the role of an *arbiter elegantiarum* at the royal court.

There is an album miniature which depicts Murad IV at a nocturnal garden party[80] and includes in all likelihood an image of Silahdar Mustafa (ill.). The miniature has been dated at approximately 1639. We see the sultan solemnly sitting on a golden throne, wearing a green sable fur-lined sur-kaftan over a red robe, holding a goblet in his left and a ceremonial handkerchief in his right hand. On his right, a cupbearer stands by with a longneck-bottle of glass filled with water, suggesting the same contents in the ruler's jewelled chalice,[81] while a few steps further in the foreground stands an official sporting a light-brown beard and a red ermine fur-lined sur-kaftan over a green robe, his hands respectfully joined (a gesture called *el pençe*). The luxurious ermine clearly classifies him as a high-ranking dignitary. This person must be Silahdar Mustafa, since all other persons in the picture, except the ruler and a bearded lute-player (Şeştârî Murad? v. i.) in front of the pasha, belong to the service staff including the sword-bearer and two dwarfs. The depiction of the official's apparel complementary to the attire of the sultan might allude to the pasha's status as a kind of *alter ego* of the monarch. In the central foreground stands a low metal table decorated with flowers in vases (mainly tulips and carnations), fruits (partly in Chinese porcelain vessels) and two burning candles. The miniature must have been produced

79 D. 3194, fol. 53b. The entry is not dated, but might refer to 1636–7. On 16 March 1637 another acquisition of shoes is mentioned: 32 pairs of boots, 35 pairs of normal shoes, 47 pairs of *mest*, 53 pairs of indoor slippers and 11 pairs of *Çerkesî*; ibidem, fol. 72.

80 The miniature in the album (*murakka*), library of the Topkapı Sarayı, Hazine 2148, fol. 11b, has been identified and dated by Ivan Stchoukine, *La peinture turque d'apres les manuscrits illustrés*. II, *De Murad IV à Mustafa III, 1623–1773*. Paris: Geuthner, 1971, p. 44 # 16 (and pl. 1), as a likeness of Murad IV.

81 Obviously Murad IV wanted to be perceived like this, given that he had banned tobacco and coffee, not to mention the religiously forbidden wine. The shape of the drinking vessel indicates a development towards more pronounced stemware since the early years of the 17th century when the turning away from the flattish bowl of earlier times prominently commenced.

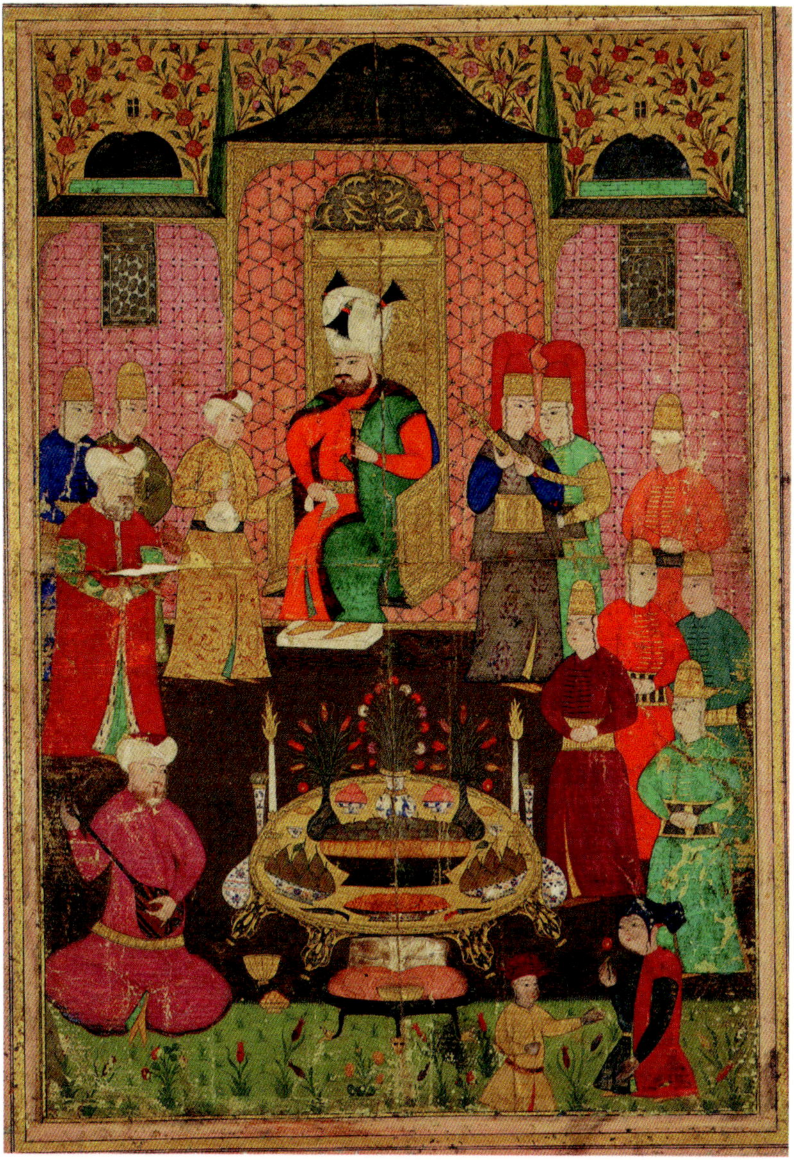

Murad IV at a nocturnal garden party, Album (*Murakka*), Istanbul, Library of the Topkapı Sarayı Müzesi, Hazine 2148, fol. 11b. (Courtesy of the Topkapı Palace Museum).

in the royal workshops, but we do not know who the painters were. An artist mentioned in our second 'brief' register as *nakkaş kadı* ('painter judge') was possibly involved. He appears once as the recipient of a turban muslin (*dülbend*) and at another time as the deliverer of *tuğras* (*tûrâ* in the document) and illuminator of a section of the Koran.[82] So he was definitively a court artist.

A favourite palace for the favourite

In 1635, when Silahdar Mustafa's meteoric rise commenced, the monarch assigned to his favourite (*musahib*) the newly furnished former palace of Makbul/Maktul İbrahim Pasha at the Hippodrome in Istanbul as Mustafa's future abode.[83] Mustafa Pasha also possessed three farms (*çiftlik*), one at the Gate to Silivri (Silivrikapı, today an urban part of Istanbul's Fatih quarter),[84] one in Alaşehir in the province of Aydın[85] and the third in the region of Balıkesir.[86]

He was probably only three years senior of his lord and the relationship between the two young men, Murad IV and Mustafa, resembled very much the intimate friendship between Süleyman the Magnificent and Makbul İbrahim Pasha. So this allusion would certainly have been intended when Murad IV endowed his friend with İbrahim Pasha's magnificent vast palace. It must have been Mustafa's charm, his eloquence, his perfect manners and his sharing many of the ruler's interests which made him the sultan's favourite. The Venetian source quoted by Hammer claims that Mustafa Pasha did not have aspirations to the grand vizierate. This would suggest he preferred to use his influence in the

82 D. 2014, fols. 9b (28 December 1639) and 15b (23 January 1640).

83 *Târih-i Na'îmâ* II, p. 824. A part of the palace was, since Maktul İbrahim Pasha's execution, used for the accommodation and training of the royal pages; Semavi Eyice, "İbrahim Paşa Sarayı", *Türkiye Diyanet Vakfı İslâm Ansiklopedisi.* (Henceforth: *DİA*) 21, Istanbul 2000, p. 345. This is also palpable in D. 3194, fol. 41b.

84 D. 3194, fol. 79b. Göyünç, "Eski Malatya'da Silâhdar Mustafa Paşa Hanı", p. 78.

85 D. 3194, fol. 58a. 29 slaves worked on the farm in Alaşehir, 19 were Russian males, four were black males, two black females and four Russian females.

86 D. 2014, fol. 13b. D. 3194, fol. 43a.

background rather than seeking to achieve a level of visible power like that enjoyed by İbrahim Pasha in his good days, eventually paying for it with his life.

Sultan Murad was not a feeble ruler; the brutality of his reign has been explained as an endeavour to establish sultanic legitimacy through an unpredictable use of power.[87] His ban on coffeehouses, on wine drinking and smoking tobacco, personally controlled in disguise with nightly tours of inspection became legendary. One might suspect that Silahdar Mustafa would accompany his lord on these excursions, but our records are silent on this aspect.

A hypochondriac and his ailing patron

The pasha would frequently call in various doctors (*hekim*),[88] surgeons to draw blood[89] and an ophthalmologist, Master Ca'fer, to cure his eye problems.[90] Mustafa's relations to the court's chief physician (*hekimbaşı*) Emir Efendi were evidently of a merely formal nature. Although pasha and physician were anything but friends, Emir Efendi would regularly receive complimentary gifts.[91] Strangely enough, not a single counter gift by Emir Efendi is recorded, possibly due to the strained relationship between the two courtiers.

Silahdar Mustafa had intended to place a protégé in the office of court physician but was rebuffed by Emir Efendi. Thereupon the pasha disclosed to the sultan in 1638 that his head physician was an opium addict, and Murad IV urged Emir Efendi to swallow a lethal overdose.[92]

Maybe Silahdar Mustafa was a hypochondriac. After all, he hoarded a whole range of bezoar (*panzehir*) stones, which were believed to pro-

87 Christoph K. Neumann in Klaus Kreiser – Christoph K. Neumann, *Kleine Geschichte der Türkei.* Stuttgart: Philipp Reclam jun., 2003, p. 206.
88 D. 525, fols. 9b, 12a, 12b, 15a, 16b, 69a, 79b. D. 2014, fols. 2a, 2b, 3a, 3b, 4a, 4b, 14b.
89 D. 525, fol. 12a. D.2014, fols. 2b, 3b.
90 D. 2014, fols. 3b, 4b, 5a.
91 D. 525, fols. 3b, 5a, 5b, 7a, 9a, 11a,70b, 71b, 82b, 89b.
92 Ayşegül Demirhan Erdemir, "Emîr Çelebi", *DİA* 11, Istanbul 1995, p. 129.

tect their owners from poisoning and were used as a remedy for many diseases. The most expensive stones were of porcupine origin, fetching a market price of forty times their own weight in gold. Also highly priced were stones deriving from monkeys (up to more than 650 times their own weight in silver), followed by those from wild hogs. The *lapis bezoar orientalis* came allegedly from wild goats in Persia and was as valuable as a jewel.[93] Two of Mustafa Pasha's bezoars were, albeit small, precious monkey stones. It was, however, an unspecified bezoar stone and probably not one of these valuable pieces which, in November 1639, was given to the sultan when he had fallen ill in Üsküdar, nor was it either of the two other stones mentioned in the entry tagged with the comment "both tested and [their healing effect] proven".[94] In December 1639, when Murad IV's condition was almost at its final stage, Silahdar Mustafa brought him two bezoar stones "from the room of the intendant of the customs in the seashore residence (*yalı*)".[95] Thus, it is not clear, whether these pieces were owned by the pasha or the customs' intendant, who twice sent bezoars to Mustafa Pasha.

Two of the pasha's bezoars were set in gold and could be worn on armbands (*pazubend*). Besides his remarkable collection of bezoars, the pasha possessed two small pieces of rhinoceros horn (*gergedan boynuzı*),[96] certainly for medical (aphrodisiac?) purposes.

It might not be by chance that the admiralty of Tersane was the place where Silahdar Mustafa handed over several of his bezoars and his pieces of rhinoceros horn to the keepers of his treasury and where he once took such stones out of a small chest (*çekmece*).[97] The port of the Maritime Arsenal formed the starting and the terminal point of Ottoman ships sailing in the eastern Mediterranean. They sometimes loaded freight from Egypt, the major transhipment point for goods from India,

93 Peter Borschberg, "The Euro-Asian Trade in Bezoar Stones (appox. 1500 to 1700)", Michael North (ed.), *Artistic and Cultural Exchanges between Europe and Asia, 1400–1900*. Franham, Surrey: Ashgate, 2010, pp. 29–43, esp. 34–35.

94 D. 2014, fol. 15b.

95 D. 2014, fol. 15b.

96 D. 2014, fol. 15b.

97 D. 2014, fol. 15b.

South East and East Asia as well as East Africa for the Levant and Europe. Captains of trading vessels had to win over the authorities of the port called at by means of customary gifts – usually a small percentage of the commodities. Thus, the presence of exotic items in Tersane (and in the hands of the customs' intendant) seems a quite natural phenomenon.

Mustafa Pasha's downfall and execution

After his master's death on 8 February 1640 and Sultan İbrahim's accession to the throne, Silahdar Mustafa was removed from the Ottoman capital, becoming governor-general of Buda and a few days later (22 Şevval 1049/22 February 1640) governor-general of Rumelia. Around that time several of his precious possessions were confiscated.[98] Although Naima writes that Mustafa was already transferred in Zilka'de of that year (23 February–24 March 1640) to Temesvar,[99] this assignment could not have occurred until around the beginning of 1641.[100] According to our second 'brief' register, the order to move to Buda was issued to Silahdar Mustafa Pasha on 17 February 1640 by the grand vizier's *kapucılar kethüdası* (deputy of the head of the porte chamberlains), who received in turn one purse (*kese*) of 50,000 *akçe* and a "royal" (*hassa*) robe of honour.[101] This response attests to Mustafa Pasha attitude that rules of protocol had to be followed even in bad times.

The state's grip on Silahdar Mustafa's treasures is indirectly reflected in his inventory. He had 30 padlocks (*kilit*) bought for 900 *akçe*, which were later supplemented with another lock costing only 10 *akçe*.[102] On 1 February 1640, exactly one week prior to Murad's passing away, the pasha's staff would pack valuables, such as jewellery, exquisite vessels

98 *Târih-i Na'îmâ* II, p. 945. Göyünç, "Eski Malatya'da Silâhdar Mustafa Paşa Hanı", p. 72, quotes a document from 26 February 1640 naming 62 camels, the dye-house and the stamp-tax (*damga mukata'ası*) of Kayseri being confiscated.

99 *Târih-i Na'îmâ* II, p. 945.

100 Göyünç, "Eski Malatya'da Silâhdar Mustafa Paşa Hanı", p. 73.

101 D. 2014, fol. 15a; fol. 13b: 18 February 1640.

102 D. 2014, fol. 5a.

bedecked with precious stones, sable fur squares (*tahta*)[103] and purses of gold coins into baskets and large haircloth sacks for grain.[104] This suggests that Mustafa was aware of the sultan's end within just a few days and obviously had no illusions as to what this would mean for his own fate. Naima reports that, on the morning after Murad IV's death, after the ceremonial oath of allegiance to the new sultan, İbrahim, Silahdar Pasha and Deli Hüseyin Pasha (also a boon companion of the deceased ruler) stepped aside and wept bitterly, as they both knew that their *dolce vita* was over.[105]

The main agent for Mustafa's downfall and eventual execution was the grand vizier, Kemankeş Kara Mustafa,[106] who was eager to have a dangerous rival out of the way. Although, once his patron was dead, Silahdar Mustafa's removal from the centre of Ottoman power was only a matter of days it took the grand vizier two full years to send him to his doom. So Silahdar's power base did not collapse like a house of cards but proved to have strong foundations. The dismissal and demotion of the governor-general of Aleppo, Kurşuncu Mehmed Pasha, a former *kethüda* (steward) and protégé of Silahdar Mustafa, on 11 November 1641,[107] was probably not an isolated case; rather, it can be seen as one of many steps to rout the influence of the former sword bearer.

The immediate cause of Mustafa's violent death was a manoeuvre by one of his clients, Mevkufatçı Mehmed Efendi.[108] This man was the major-domo of Murad IV's little daughter Kaya Sultan (born in 1632

---

[103] Sable fur was a much favoured gift in the upper echelons of Ottoman society. It was usually given in the form of squares (*tahta*) sewn together from pieces matching in colour, origin and quality, similar to "plates" in the terminology of modern furriery. The term *tahta* does not refer to a particular size; cf. Hülya Tezcan, "Furs and skins owned by the Sultans", Suraiya Faroqhi – Christoph K. Neumann (eds.), *Ottoman Costumes: From Textile to Identity*. Istanbul: Eren, 2004, p. 66.

[104] D. 2014, fol. 16b.

[105] *Târih-i Na'îmâ* II, p. 942–3.

[106] *Târih-i Na'îmâ* III, p. 957.

[107] Rhoads Murphey, *Exploring Ottoman Sovereignty: Tradition, Image and Practice in the Ottoman Imperial Households, 1400–1800*. London-New York: Continuum, 2008, p. 255.

[108] He is once mentioned in the second 'brief' register as bringing a cash gift from Silahdar Mustafa Pasha, D. 2014, fol. 3b.

or 1633)[109], with whom Mustafa had been betrothed when she was still a toddler. In an attempt to bring Silahdar Mustafa to power again Mevkufatçı Mehmed, together with other devotees of the pasha, planned to arrange his marriage with the little princess. This was intended to secure, in the long run, a post such as *kaymakam* (deputy grand vizier) or even the grand vizierate for Silahdar Mustafa. The retainers found a way to convince the *valide sultan* (Kösem Mahpeyker, who was anyhow protecting the pasha[110]) to support the marriage plan.[111] Finally, in 1642, grand vizier Kemankeş Kara Mustafa Pasha obtained a death sentence for the former favourite of Sultan Murad, although, according to Schmid's report, he was to pay for it with the bitter enmity of the *valide sultan*, which led two years later to his, Kemankeş's, own execution.[112]

Apparently, Silahdar Mustafa eventually fell victim to a wider power struggle, a covert battle between the grand vizier and the domineering mother of the sultan. This may be supported by Naima's report that one of Kösem Mahpeyker's ladies-in-waiting, who was a partisan (*cânibgîr*) of Silahdar and informed her mistress about his situation, was strangled.[113] Strangely enough, however, Silahdar Mustafa's ties with Kösem Mahpeyker are not noticeably reflected in the registers.

The external cause for the persecution and eventual execution of Silahdar Mustafa was his wealth, in particular his income from the public treasury of Cyprus, amounting to 80,000 *guruş* per year,[114] an income he had been pocketing since September 1635, when the sultan allocated him the poll tax (*cizye*) of Cyprus as a reward for his military accomplishments at the siege of Baghdad.[115] In our 'brief' registers the financial link with Cyprus is not only suggested by gifts from several

---

109 M. Çağatay Uluçay, *Padişahların Kadınları ve Kızları*. Ankara: TTK 1980, p. 54.
110 Cf. Mücteba İlgürel, "Kösem Sultan", *DİA* 26, Ankara 2002, p. 274.
111 *Târih-i Na'îmâ* III, pp. 956–957.
112 Meienberger, *Johann Rudolf Schmid zum Schwarzenhorn*, p. 69, note 50. *Târih-i Na'îmâ* III, p. 957.
113 *Târih-i Na'îmâ* III, p. 958.
114 *Târih-i Na'îmâ* III, p. 956.
115 Göyünç, "Eski Malatya'da Silâhdar Mustafa Paşa Hanı", pp. 70–71.

governor-generals of the island,[116] but also by an entry attesting the arrival of its treasury.[117]

The *bostancıbaşı* ('head gardener', who was in charge with the execution of high-ranking officials) of Edirne, Sinan Ağa, was sent with a *ferman* to Temesvar, and the pasha was imprisoned in the fortress to force him to surrender his assets. Cash and valuables, in total worth 50,000 *guruş*, were collected. After Silahdar Mustafa declared that he was not capable of producing any more, a death sentence was obtained,[118] and Sinan Ağa did his job with the help of "forty merciless *bostancı*-executioners" in the fortress of Temesvar.[119]

According to Naima, cash and precious goods, in total worth "5,000 purses" (*kese*) were collected after Mustafa Pasha's death.[120] A document referring to Silahdar Mustafa Pasha's cash assets, dated 8 Muharrem 1052 (8 April 1642), lists 21 purses of 'mixed' (*mahlut*) *gurus*, which "were handed over by Beşir Ağa to the *harem*" (*Beşir Ağa yediyle hareme teslim olunmuşdur*); three purses of *para*, six purses of *kara akçe* and eleven purses of *çil akçe* were taken into the treasury. An explanation in the record states that it had originally been 42 purses, and eleven purses of *çil akçe* had been taken in (*içerüye*).[121]

The contemporary chronicle of the secretary of the artillery (*topçular kâtibi*), Abdülkadir (Kadrî) Efendi, reports that all effects and the palace of Mustafa Pasha were put under seal and that the senior treasurer of the *enderun* (inner palace) was assigned to confiscate the bequest and hand it over to the royal *harem*.[122] The fact that indeed a part of Silahdar Mustafa's cash assets was given to the royal *harem* corroborates the suspicion that the power struggle to which the pasha had fallen victim was being fought out between the royal ladies as well.

116 D. 525, fols. 10a (İbrahim Pasha, 9 November 1637), 70a (Ali Pasha, 8 August 1636). D. 2014, fol. 13a (Halil Pasha, 23 November 1639).

117 D. 525, fol 79b (the man of Ali Pasha's household bringing the treasury money of Cyprus received 10,000 *akçe*, 26 May 1636).

118 *Târih-i Na'îmâ* III, p. 956.

119 *Târih-i Na'îmâ* III, p. 957.

120 *Târih-i Na'îmâ* III, p. 956.

121 TSMA, D. 10535, fol. 1b.

122 *'Abdülkādir Efendi Tarihi.* II, p. 1162.

Mustafa Pasha's child bride Kaya Sultan

Silihdar Mustafa's distant relationship to Murad IV's little daughter Kaya Sultan is perceptible in our registers. Later she became the beloved wife of Evliya Çelebi's uncle Melek Ahmed Pasha and object of Evliya's adoration. In 1659 she died in childbirth. Evliya gives a detailed account of her gruesome death.[123]

On 16 July 1639, when she was six or seven years old, she was pampered with a jewelled golden flask (*altun murassaʿ matara*) Silahdar Mustafa had bought in Diyarbekir.[124] For the following *Şeker Bayramı* (Sugar Feast) the little princess received (18 January 1640) one dress-length of *londura çuka,*[125] while two of the ruler's *hassekis* (favourite concubines)[126] and the *kethüda kadın* (female steward) of the imperial *harem* were treated with analogous gifts. Of course, the *valide sultan* also belonged to the recipients of holiday presents: much like Kaya Sultan, the two *hassekis* and the *kethüda kadın,* she obtained two lengths of serge (*saye çuka*) on 22 January 1640.[127] As Silahdar Mustafa was well versed in all matters of ceremonial, we may understand the offering of two length of broadcloth to each of the royal ladies as a polite courtesy with no anticipation of a counter-gift or favour.

Although the marriage to a royal princess required the divorce of all previous wives and separation from concubines, this was unlikely to have been expected over the period in which the future royal son-in-law had to wait until his child bride was nubile. Indeed, Mustafa Pasha had

---

123 Robert Dankoff (trsl.), *The Intimate Life of an Ottoman Statesman: Melek Ahmed Pasha (1588–1662) as portrayed in Evliya Çelebi's Book of Travels (Seyahat-name).* Albany, N.Y.: SUNY, 1991, pp. 230–231.

124 D. 2014, 10a. Possibly, a share of the grand vizier's gifts to Silahdar Mustafa Pasha (2 October 1639) was allotted by the pasha to Kaya Sultan: three lengths of 'Frankish' satin (*Efrengî diba*) and three lengths of patterned brocaded velvet (for a cape) were destined for "the little princess" (*küçük sultan*), D. 2014, fol. 13a.

125 This is the Ottoman name for 'Londra', the term Italian merchants used for broadcloth from London, at that time apparently first quality; see Ralph Davis, *Aleppo and Devonshire Square: English Traders in the Levant in the Eighteenth Century.* London etc.: Macmillan, 1967, pp. 100–102.

126 Uluçay, *Padişahların Kadınları,* p. 54, names only one *hasseki,* Ayşe Sultan.

127 D. 2014, fol. 15b.

a *harem*, otherwise the acquisition of a black eunuch at 40,000 *akçe*[128] would not make sense. The same goes for a gift of female silver jewellery from the governor-general of Buda, Hüseyin Pasha in 1637.[129]

Buildings endowed by Silahdar Mustafa

A fountain built in 1048 (1638–39) by Silahdar Mustafa Pasha in Istanbul's Cihangir quarter has survived the hardships of time. Although the inscription is lost, its text (with the name of the patron) is known from the *divan* of the poet and calligrapher Cevrî İbrahim Çelebi,[130] a follower (but not necessarily a dervish) of the Mevleviye order. Our second 'brief' register reports that on 9 Receb 1049 (5 November 1639) a Mahmud Efendi, *the* calligrapher of the time,[131] was rewarded with 3,000 *akçe* for engraving the chronogram in the fountain built by our official in Cihangir.[132] The building costs (150,000 *akçe*[133]) are not listed in our *defter*, but we learn that on 24 Rebi' II 1049 (24 August 1639) Cevrî Çelebi had already received 60 *guruş* for composing a chronogram.[134] Two weeks earlier (10 August 1639), at the official seat of the admiralty

---

128 D. 525, fol. 66a.

129 D. 525, fol. 11b.

130 See http://www.suvakfi.org.tr/detay.asp?id=181 (accessed 24 September 2014). Hüseyin Ayan (ed.), *Cevrî: Hayâtı, Edebî Kişiliği, Eserleri ve Divanının Tenkidli Metni.* Erzurum 1981, pp. 300–301, XXVII. On Cevrî see Hüseyin Ayan, "Cevrî İbrahim Çelebi", *DİA* 7, Istanbul 1993, pp. 460–461. E. J. W. Gibb, *A History of Ottoman Poetry.* (henceforth: *HOP*) III, Edward G. Browne (ed.). [2]London: Luzac, 1965, pp. 297–301. As a calligrapher Cevrî was especially famed for his copies of Celâl ed-Din Rumî's *Mathnawî*; of which several copies are extant today; see Zeren Tanındı, "A Treasury for Bibliophiles: Ottoman Illuminated Books", *Distant Neighbours, Close Memories: 600 Years of Turkish-Polish Relations.* Istanbul: Sakıp Sabancı Museum, 2014, p. 98.

131 He also created the inscription on Murad IV's throne, a *kaside* by Cevrî on the conquest of Baghdad, and the Koranic verses in the Revan Köşkü, newly built in the Topkapı Palace; see Hammer, *GOR* V, p. 262 and 283.

132 D. 2014, fol. 4a: *Cihangir'de sahib-i devlet bina eyledüğe* (!) *çeşme* (!) *tarih kazduran Mahmud Efendi'ye in'am: akçe 3000, fi 9 Receb 1049* (5 November 1639), *('an yed-i kapucılar kethüdası).*

133 Göyünç, "Eski Malatya'da Silâhdar Mustafa Paşa Hanı", p. 81.

134 D. 2014, fol. 3a: *Tersane'de tarih söyleyen Cevrî Çelebi'ye in'am-ı sahib-i devlet: guruş 60, fi 24 Rebi' II 1049* (24 August 1639).

in Tersane, the pasha had paid homage to the poet by accoutring him with one dress-length of scarlet (*iskarlat çuka*) and a turban (*sarık*).[135]

The 'long' *defter* reports that on 11 May 1636 Silahdar Mustafa spent 130,000 *akçe* on the repair of a mosque or a *mescid* (mosque without a pulpit) in Tophane and made a pious foundation worth 100,000 *akçe* for this house of prayer.[136] It is unclear which mosque is meant, possibly, the Tophane Ocağı Mescidi, which was founded by Süleyman the Magnificent; yet the reference work by Ayvansarayî speaks of decay after a fire, but does not mention a repair of Silahdar Mustafa.[137] Not quite a month later he invested 360,000 *akçe* in building two fountains in that neighbourhood.[138]

Evliya mentions a *sebil* (public fountain with free distribution of water) opposite the courtyard of the Kılıç Ali Mosque. The chronogram on the inscription was again composed by Cevrî in 1636–37.[139] The structure has since disappeared. Silahdar Mustafa had a further fountain built in Fındıklı, again with a chronogram by Cevrî.[140]

To judge from the remarkable scope of his chronograms for the uppermost echelons of the empire,[141] Cevrî must have been very much

---

135 D. 2014, fol. 9b. Scarlet (Ital. *scarlatto*) was a very fine and precious woollen fabric, often dyed in a vivid scarlet.

136 D. 3194, fol. 34b. This entry calls the building a 'mosque' (*cami'*), but in the *icmal* (summarised addition) it is called a *mescid*; ibidem, fol. 35b.

137 Hafız Hüseyin Ayvansarayî, *Hadikat al-Cevami*. II. Istanbul: Matba'a-ı 'amire, 1281 (1864–5), p. 76. Howard Crane (trsl.), *The Garden of the Mosques: Hafız Hüseyin al-Ayvansarayî's Guide to the Muslim Monuments of Ottoman Istanbul*. Leiden etc.: Brill, 2000, p. 396.

138 D. 3194, fol. 35a. The entry is dated 3 June 1636 (28 Zilhicce 1035 H). For another fountain, in the village of Elma Ağaç in the province of Kütahya, he spent in October 1636 20,000 *akçe*; ibidem, fol. 37b.

139 Orhan Şaik Gökyay (ed.), *Evliya Çelebi Seyahatnâmesi*. Evliya Çelebi b. Derviş Muhammed Zıllî. 1. Kitap: İstanbul. Istanbul: YKB, 1996, pp. 189–190. Ayan (ed.), *Cevrî*, p. 300.

140 Ayan (ed.), *Cevrî*, p. 300, XXVI. Evliya Çelebi gives only the last line of the poem bearing the date; Gökyay (ed.), *Evliya Çelebi Seyahatnâmesi*. I, p. 190. Göyünç, "Eski Malatya'da Silâhdar Mustafa Paşa Hanı", p. 81. The bookkeeping in D. 3194, fol. 35a, speaks of two fountains in Tophane and notes a payment of 320,000 *akçe* for them on 23 May 1636. The issue required, however, more money: on 5 September 1636 120,000 *akçe* were again paid for the Tophane fountains, ibidem, fol. 36b.

141 Ayan (ed.), *Cevrî*, pp. 283–345. Cf. also Gibb, *HOP* III, p. 299.

in fashion with the ruling elite of his time. According to Evliya Çelebi he belonged to the circle of poets Murad IV would assemble every Sunday evening for intimate conversation (*can sohbeti*).[142] Cevrî also composed a chronogram for the enormous *kervansaray* that Silahdar Mustafa had built in 1636–37 in Malatya.[143] This inscription, originally produced for the entrance gate, seems now to be in the local museum. A second inscription, still in its original place over the entrance to the covered section of the building, has been penned by the *şeyhülislam* and poet Yahya Efendi,[144] the most eminent poet of his time.[145] The *kervansaray* was a miserable ruin for many years but has now been restored and largely rebuilt.

The 'long' register has several entries referring to the building,[146] but, as far as I can see, does not mention Yahya Efendi. Nejat Göyünç has unearthed several documents which shed light on the genesis of this colossal edifice.[147] Silahdar Mustafa's agent there was a certain Musli Ağa, who is, however, not mentioned in the 'brief' inventories, although several individuals of this name can be traced.[148]

142 Gökyay (ed.), *Evliya Çelebi Seyahatnâmesi.* I, p. 105.

143 Ayan (ed.), *Cevrî,* p. 301, XXVIII. Göyünç, "Eski Malatya'da Silâhdar Mustafa Paşa Hanı", p. 90.

144 Cf. Bayram Ali Kaya, "Yahyâ Efendi, Zekeriyyâzâde", *DİA* 43, İstanbul 2013, pp. 245–246. For the text of the inscription see Göyünç, "Eski Malatya'da Silâhdar Mustafa Paşa Hanı", p. 90.

145 Cf. Gibb, *HOP* III, pp. 273–284.

146 D. 3194, fols. 36a, 36b, 37b, 39a, 40a, 40b, 41a, 42b.

147 Göyünç, "Eski Malatya'da Silâhdar Mustafa Paşa Hanı", pp. 66–69 and 83–92; idem, "Silâhdar Mustafa Paşa Hanı'na Âit Bir Vesika", *İstanbul Üniversitesi Edebiyat Fakültesi Tarih Dergisi* XXV (1971), pp. 73–78. See also Erol Özbilgen, "Eski Malatya'da Silâhdar Mustafa Paşa Hanı'nın Restitüsyonu Hakkında", *İstanbul Üniversitesi Edebiyat Fakültesi Tarih Enstitüsü Dergisi* I (1970), pp. 93–102.

148 Mustafa Pasha's agent can hardly be identical with Çöğürci (choghur player) Musli Bey, referred to in the first 'brief' document; D. 525, fol. 15a and 70b. Another Musli is the lame (*topal*) *şatır* (running attendant), an office which makes it very unlikely that he would also have been employed as an agent for such an important building. Still another Musli Efendi from Bosnia, mentioned in the first 'brief' register, is identified in the second record as finance director (*defterdar*) of Bosnia; ibidem, fol. 72b; D. 2014, fol. 12b. A further Musli Çelebi, referred to in the second register as a maker or seller of printed cotton fabric (*basmacı*), seems not to be a good candidate either (ibidem, fol. 3a).

Whereabouts of Silahdar Mustafa

While the first 'brief' *defter* has only very occasionally concealed hints about the pasha's activities, the second 'brief' record discloses much more. Not all entries are provided with dates and place names, hence sometimes we are left in the dark as to when and where something happened. Nevertheless, we can extract from the documents one remarkable feature of our hero: he was almost constantly on the move. He was present at the Baghdad campaign (April 1638 – end of May 1639) and accompanied his lord on the way back.[149] His military success in Baghdad can be traced in our first 'brief' register,[150] while many stops of his return journey are recorded in the second *defter*.[151] Moreover, we learn that an astrologer, Hasan Çelebi, belonged to the group of travellers.[152] Whenever an opportunity arose on the way, the pasha would go shopping: in Tokat he bought 'a little (male) slave' for 160 *guruş*, and in Ankara he had his treasurer buy several bales of the exclusive luxury fabric *sof* (mohair) for which this town was famous.[153]

149 A register listing Silahdar Mustafa's campaign treasury is extant in the archives of the Topkapı Palace, D. 9056. The register has suffered a lot and is in some parts barely readable. To take considerable quantities of textiles, luxurious weapons, horse equipment and other valuables on a campaign was not unusual for Ottoman grandees. The exchange of gifts would continue during warfare, so these items were needed. Yet usually a substantial part of the treasury would not be taken to the front but left behind in a secure place. Silahdar Mustafa stashed a number of his possessions in Diyarbakır.

150 D. 525, fol. 32b.

151 D. 2014, fol. 1b. The stops are given in this order: Kalkan, Alaca Han, Selçuk [Hanı], Tuzla, Ilıca, Sivas, Köpri (5 May 1639), Artukova (Artova, 6 May 1639), Tokat (8 May 1639), Zile (22 May 1639), Engürü (Ankara, 23 May 1639). The sequence and some of the place names are not consistent with the list given by Halil Sahillioğlu, "Dördüncü Murad'ın Bağdat seferi menzilnamesi (Bağdat seferi harp jurnalı)", *Belgeler* II, sayı 3–4 (1965), p. 10.

152 D. 2014, fol. 1b.

153 Ibidem. For the manufacturing of *sof* see Suraiya Faroqhi, "Ottoman Textiles in European Markets", Anna Contadini and Claire Norton (eds.), *The Renaissance and the Ottoman World*. Farnham, Surrey: Ashgate, 2013, pp. 237–240. A general overview of the mohair industry of Ankara is given in Suraiya Faroqhi, "Mohair Manufacture and Mohair Workshops in Seventeenth-Century Ankara", *Ord. Prof. Lütfi Barkan'a Armağan.* = *İstanbul Üniversitesi İktisat Fakültesi Mecmuası* 41/1–4 (1982–1983), pp. 211–236.

Apart from the campaign, he was permanently meandering around Istanbul, moving between the palaces and gardens of the Topkapı Sarayı,[154] the Old Palace (Eski Saray), Davudpaşa, Üsküdar (Kavak Sarayı), the garden of İstavroz (today: Beylerbeyi), of Kandilli, of Beykoz (Sultaniye), the official seat of the *kapudan paşa* (admiral) with the shipyards in Tersane at the edge of Kasımpaşa,[155] the garden of Hasan Kalfa (at the Akıntı Burnu in Arnavudköy, stretching north towards Bebek), of Sahib Hatun[156] and of Fener,[157] and rarely staying in his enormous palace at the Hippodrome.

He must have had an enormous household there. But, for the most part, our 'brief' registers do not allow us to assign the *ağas*, mutes and other staff members unambiguously to his or the sultan's entourage. Only his pages, called 'little boys' (*oğlancık*) in the registers, were clearly part of his personal retinue.[158] They were evidently an indication of elevated status, as they would accompany the pasha on many of his trips from one end of Istanbul to the other.[159] Evidently this continuous changing of places issued not so much from the pasha's own will; he simply followed his restless lord, Murad IV.

[154] The Topkapı Palace is not explicitly mentioned, but there are several references to "the royal garden" (*bağçe-i hassa*), a term which denotes every garden possessed by the sultan. Yet, since it is once indirectly linked to İstanbul (D. 525, fol. 79b), the "royal garden" signifies here in all likelihood the one around the Topkapı Palace.

[155] It is not easy to tell apart the palace and the shipyards, as both are referred to as Tersane. As Tersane is mentioned only after Silahdar Mustafa Pasha became admiral of the fleet, the term refers probably only to the shipyards and the offices of the *kapudan*. For the dockyards and the seat of the admiralty see Wolfgang Müller-Wiener, "Zur Geschichte des Tersâne-i Âmire in Istanbul", Jean-Louis Bacqué-Grammont et al. (eds.), *Türkische Miszellen: Robert Anhegger Festschrift, Armağanı, Mélanges*. Istanbul: Editions Divit Press, 1987, pp. 253–258 and 268–269.

[156] Unfortunately I could not localise this garden, and it is not mentioned in Muzaffer Erdoğan, "Osmanlı Devrinde İstanbul Bahçeleri", *Vakıflar Dergisi* IV (1958), pp. 149–182, and in the relevant literature.

[157] See Erdoğan, "Osmanlı Devrinde İstanbul Bahçeleri", p. 174–175.

[158] The pasha took care for their education; on 3 June 1636, for example, paper and inkwells were bought for them; D. 3194, fol. 35a.

[159] D. 2014, fols. 2b, 3a, 4b, 5a. After Murad IV's death at least some of the pages would escort him to Sofya; ibidem, fol. 10b.

Gardens as places of distraction

Frequent outings to suburban gardens had been an old practice for Ottoman rulers. Regular short day trips (*biniş-i hümayun*) are, for example, reported for Süleyman the Magnificent.[160]

To seek entertainment and distraction in gardens was not a specific feature of Murad IV's reign. It had a long tradition, particularly in the Persianate world, and was a favoured topic in poetry.[161] Our registers represent a significant complement to literary sources, as they provide us with valuable insights into this aspect of social life in the real world.

Poets and musicians were in general indispensable elements of drinking parties under the open sky. In addition to the feasting, the pleasures the sultan and his boon companions would enjoy in a garden were well-established: hunting, archery, wrestling, firework displays, and sometimes performances of acrobatics.[162] We are able to trace all these activities, except the last one, in a rather personal way in our records.

The first, unfortunately undated, entries of the earlier 'brief' register deal with tents (*otaklar*), manufactured in Aleppo. The main structure had as many as ten poles, a mosquito net (*namusiye*) and a wax-cloth cover (*muşamma*').[163] This cover was usually sea-green; to achieve this hue copper chloride was used and to protect the structure against rain gum Arabic was applied. The marquee must have served as the pasha's assembly and reception room (*divan*), since so many poles (even when positioned in a double row) suggest an enormous tent. Additionally, a smaller tent, *çerge*, with only three poles is mentioned, again made of

---

160 Gülru Necipoğlu, "The Suburban Landscape of Sixteenth-Century Istanbul as a Mirror of Classical Ottoman Garden Culture", Attilio Petruccioli (ed.), *Gardens in the Time of the Great Muslim Empires: Theory and Design*. Leiden-New York-Köln, 1997, p. 33.

161 Cf. Halil İnalcık, *Has-bağçede 'Ayş u Tarab: Nedimler, Şâirler, Mutribler*. Istanbul: İş Bankası, 2011.

162 Murat Yıldız, "Padişahların Dinlenme ve Eğlenme Mekânları: İstanbul Bahçeleri", Feridun M. Emecen, Ali Akyıldız, Emrah Safa Gürkan (eds.), *Osmanlı İstanbulu*. (Uluslarası Osmanlı İstanbulu Sempozyumu II, 2014). Istanbul: 29 Mayıs Universitesi – İstanbul Büyükşehir Belediyesi, 2014, vol. II, pp. 660–669.

163 D. 525, fol. 1b.

wax-cloth. The whole tentage was fenced with an enclosure adorned with *mihrabs* (prayer niches).[164] The 'long' register lists on 19 April 1636 another range of newly made tents which must have been predominantly destined for Mustafa Pasha's retinue; the considerable sum of 426,151 *akçe* was spent for these structures.[165]

In status-conscious Ottoman society a certain rank would be demonstrated in material culture by diverse means, including tents and tent equipment. Thus, an enclosure for tentage was a clear indication of high rank; a remark in the memoirs of Alexander Mavrokordatos, *divan* dragoman and adviser in foreign politics to Merzifonlu Kara Mustafa Pasha, implies that *sancakbeys* (governors of sub-provinces) were not entitled to use fences.[166] Given that Silahdar Mustafa's endowment activity started in 1636, shortly after he reached the rank of vizier, which was advertised in the respective inscriptions, the ordering of stately tents in Aleppo must be seen as another means to broadcast his new status. On 19 July 1637 a stable tent (*ahur çergesi*) with three poles was acquired for 41,300 *akçe*, obviously to accommodate the pasha's horses.[167] This was not only due to practical needs, but also to indicate his growing eminence.

---

164 Jürg Rageth (Basel) in a paper read at the Volkmanntreffen on 25 October 2014 ("Princely Tent Hangings with Niche Design – from Late Antiquity to the Modern Age and from Marocco to Central Asia") showed convincingly that niche designs in tent enclosures were a symbol of sovereignty and power.

165 D. 3194, fol. 103b. 19 tents (*çerge*) with 16 *hazine* (panel), 11 tents (*çadır*) with 12 *hazine*, 45 tents (*çadır*) with ten *hazine*, 45 tents (*çadır*) with eight *hazine*, two kitchen tents (*çerge-i matbah*), one tent (*çerge*) for the treasurer, two privy tents with seven *hazine* each (one for the pasha himself and one for his slaves), one *hamam* tent (made of broadcloth, *çuka*, which was taken from the treasury), two larder tents and one tent (*oba*) for the pasha's steward are listed; we already mentioned the tent with mosquito net for Mustafa Pasha's brother Mahmud, which was part of the newly made tentage. For *hazine* (panel) see Nurhan Atasoy, *Otağ-ı Hümayun: Osmanlı Çadırları*. Istanbul: Aygaz, 2000, p. 19.

166 Mavrokordatos reports that the pasha, after his escape from the disaster before Vienna, had to spend the night in the tent of a *sancakbey* which did not have enclosures; Richard F. Kreutel, *Kara Mustafa vor Wien: 1683 aus der Sicht türkischer Quellen.* Karl Teply (ed.), Graz-Wien-Köln: Styria, 1982, p. 90.

167 D. 3194, fol. 40a.

A few hints in the registers suggest that, during the good season, Mustafa Pasha and his lord would camp in their tents in the gardens.[168] Silahdar Mustafa's acquisition of palatial tents points to sojourns in great style. As all the sites mentioned had solid buildings, tentage evidently served to radiate extra splendour.

Davudpaşa[169] and Üsküdar (Kavak Sarayı)[170] were real palaces. The site of Üsküdar had been furnished with some additions (particularly a domed kiosk commemorating the conquest of Jerevan in 1635[171]) during the late years of Murad IV, maybe partly as a gift by his favourite Silahdar Mustafa Pasha.[172] It seems to have not been uncommon for viziers close to the ruler to adorn a royal garden with supplementary structures. The palace of Üsküdar had a pavilion (*kasr*) of Mehmed Pasha, which had apparently been erected by Selim II's grand vizier and son-in-law Sokollu Mehmed Pasha.[173]

On an unknown date, probably in the course of the year 1637, Silahdar Mustafa paid 44,300 *kara akçe* for the construction of a kitchen

---

168 D. 525, fol. 11b, refers to the sultan's move to the tents on 23 April 1638; fol. 26a, notes money coming to the treasurer in Üsküdar "on the day when the prosperous sultan moved into his tent". A gift package from the Kaimakam Kapudan Pasha [Kemankeş Kara Mustafa] came on 13 April 1638, when the sultan moved into his tent, fol. 27b. Ibidem, fol. 14b, records a substantial gratuity of 10,000 *akçe* for the tent pitchers (*çadır mehterler*) on 19 July 1637 in Üsküdar. D. 2014, fol. 4a, mentions half a *guruş* for transporting the tents in Beykoz to the landing stage.

169 Cf. Semavi Eyice, "Davud Paşa Sarayı" *Dünden Bugüne İstanbul Ansiklopedisi.* III. Istanbul: Kültür Bakanlığı/Tarih Vakfı, 1994, pp. 8–9. Tülay Artan, "Davutpaşa Bahçesi", ibidem, pp. 10–11.

170 Cf. Wolfgang Müller-Wiener, "Das Kavak Sarayı – ein verlorenes Baudenkmal Istanbuls", *Istanbuler Mitteilungen* 38 (1988), pp. 363–376. Tülay Artan – Christoph K. Neumann, "Kavak Sarayı", *İstanbul Ansiklopedisi.* IV, pp. 494–495. Nurhan Atasoy, *A Garden for the Sultan: Gardens and flowers in the Ottoman culture.* [Istanbul]: Aygaz, 2002, pp. 310–314 (with several illustrations). D. 525, fol. 10a, records a red *mukaddem* belt, Silahdar Mustafa brought to the kiosk (*köşk*) of Üsküdar to the sultan.

171 Necipoğlu, "The Suburban Landscape", p. 36.

172 Although the register does not explicitly state that the building activity of this time in Üsküdar was carried out in the royal gardens of the Kavak Palace, there are no indications in the registers of property in this area being owned by Silahdar Mustafa, which suggests a gift of the pasha on the palace grounds. Undertakings of this kind fit perfectly into the Ottoman patterns of gifting and courtly generosity.

173 Necipoğlu, "The Suburban Landscape", p. 36.

in Üsküdar;[174] on 11 March 1637 he gave 1,860 *akçe* for a pavement (*kaldırım*) there,[175] on 18 May 1637 he spent 74,564 *akçe* for a *hamam* to be built in these gardens,[176] and on 23 July 1637 he laid out 100 *guruş* (12,000 *akçe*) for labourers' wages and lime for the erection of a new portal (*kapı*) at the Üsküdar gardens, which cost him another 275 *guruş* (33,000 *akçe*) a month later (28 August 1637).[177] In a similar way Silahdar Mustafa took a share in the costs of mortar and timber for the chambers (*odalar*) which were added to the palace of Davudpaşa.[178] Offering a building as a gift to one's lord was not uncommon in Ottoman society at the time; Silahdar Mustafa himself received a *han* near Manisa as a present from one of his clients, Mahmud Ağa.[179]

Archival evidence suggests that the palace of Üsküdar was laid out only for recreation and lacked any units for administrative purposes.[180] This feature was even more apparent at İstavroz,[181] Kandilli,[182] Hasan Kalfa[183] and Fener Bahçesi,[184] all sites possessing only small structures and garden pavilions. For the garden of Kandilli, a piece of furniture is once mentioned: a wooden *taht*,[185] a kind of bench in the form of a modern bedstead, still used for socialising in southeastern Turkey, Iran and Central Asia.

In 1528–29 a complete palace was built in the Sultaniye garden of Beykoz, although it is described by Du Fresne-Canaye in 1573 as a small ensemble. The residential structures were largely built of wood, and although the place served ceremonial purposes in Süleyman the Mag-

174 D. 525, fol. 4a. The entry is not dated.
175 D. 525, fol. 72a.
176 D. 525, fol. 12b.
177 D. 525, fol. 14b.
178 D. 525, fol. 15a.
179 Göyünç, "Eski Malatya'da Silâhdar Mustafa Paşa Hanı", p. 79.
180 Necipoğlu, "The Suburban Landscape", p. 36.
181 Atasoy, *A Garden for the Sultan*, pp. 315–316.
182 Atasoy, *A Garden for the Sultan*, pp. 318–320.
183 Atasoy, *A Garden for the Sultan*, pp. 302–303.
184 Atasoy, *A Garden for the Sultan*, pp. 307–309. Tülay Artan, "Fener Bahçesi", *İstanbul Ansiklopedisi.* III, pp. 281–282. Eadem, "Fener Köşkü", ibidem, pp. 282–283.
185 D. 2014, fol. 2b.

nificent's time,[186] its status is unclear in Murad IV's days. When Silahdar Mustafa and his lord were visiting in November 1639, they apparently stayed in tents.[187] As the forests and hills behind the garden were full of game, in particular boar,[188] the sojourn was in all likelihood dedicated to hunting. Perhaps, this garden (and several others) had once come into being as a hunting park. Evliya Çelebi calls it a paradisal rose garden (*gülistan*) with cypresses and other trees. He claims it had been built by Bayezid II and relates that Özdemiroğlu Osman Pasha had supplied luxurious building materials, such as a dome, windows, panes, roofs and shutters to Murad III, and that an 'Edenic' pavilion (*kasr*) had been erected. Its walls were mainly painted with hunting scenes.[189]

The complex of Davudpaşa apparently not only contained accommodation for the whole royal family and the service staff but might well have been equipped with facilities for the tasks of government to be performed.[190] According to Naima, Persian ambassador Maksud Khan, who arrived on 9 August 1637 at Üsküdar, was accommodated in Davudpaşa, whereupon he was confined and closely-guarded there during the Baghdad campaign.[191] Although, our documents speak time and again of a *göç-i Davudpaşa* (move to Davudpaşa), the visits there usually lasted only a few days. So the strict confinement of Maksud Khan in one of the palace's buildings might also indicate that the place was not one of the sultan's favourite abodes.

The pasha's frequent trips in 1639 to his official seat, the admiralty of Tersane, were not only necessary for tasks which could not be accomplished anywhere else, but also because most gardens and parks

---

[186] Necipoğlu, "The Suburban Landscape", pp. 37–38.

[187] D. 2014, fol. 4a, 9b, 10a/b.

[188] Philippe du Fresne-Canaye, *Le Voyage du Levant*. M. H. Hauser (ed.), Paris: Ernest Leroux, 1897 (reprint: Frankfurt/Main: Institute for the History of Arabic-Islamic Science, 1995), p. 88. Necipoğlu, "The Suburban Landscape", p. 37.

[189] Gökyay (ed.), *Evliya Çelebi Seyahatnâmesi*. I, p. 199.

[190] Cf. Sedad Hakkı Eldem, *Köşkler ve Kasırlar*. I, Istanbul: Devlet Güzel Sanatlar Akademisi, 1969, p. 210. Eldem quotes an undated document (which he attributes to the late 17th century, though) suggesting various residential and administrative units.

[191] *Târih-i Na'îmâ* II, p. 857. Eldem, *Köşkler*, p. 210.

had only small summer houses without the infrastructure needed for administrative duties.

It was not only the royal gardens that the pasha would visit but also the garden of Ebusu‘ud, where a soiree took place,[192] or the garden of İbrahim Çelebi, where Silahdar Mustafa arrived by boat.[193] A Ma‘cuncı Garden is once mentioned and the wording leaves open the possibility that our pasha was the owner,[194] although this seems to be a weak assumption. The famous Karabalizade Garden between Kabataş and Beşiktaş, which has been depicted and described by Salomon Schweigger as a “Lustgarten” (pleasure garden) in the eighties of the 16th century,[195] is also mentioned because a gardener brought Silahdar Mustafa some radish from there.[196]

This reference does not imply, however, that this land had since been turned into a vegetable garden; for a combination of trees, flower and vegetable beds were a typical feature of Ottoman garden culture from the early days.[197] Indeed, the tradition of combining a kitchen garden with pleasure grounds reaches back to antiquity.[198] One reason for its continuation might have been to mask a somewhat frivolous venue with a more utilitarian face.

A further garden, spelled Murattıb (probably erroneously for *mutrıb*, “musician”) Mustafa Çelebi Bahçesi, is referred to. This one, which might have had an owner from the urban middleclass, was apparently also used to grow not only ornamental plants but also vegetables.[199]

---

192 D. 2014, fol. 2b.

193 D. 2014, fol. 3b. This garden of İbrahim Çelebi was probably owned by Defterdarzade İbrahim Çelebi, v. i.

194 D. 2014, fol. 5a.

195 Salomon Schweigger, *Ein newe Reyßbeschreibung auß Teutschland Nach Constantinopel und Jerusalem*. Nürnberg: Johann Lantzenberger, 1608; reprint: Graz: Akademische Druck- u. Verlagsanstalt, 1964, pp. 126–127. This garden was one of the rare examples of a Persianate *chahārbāgh* layout in Ottoman garden culture, cf. Necipoğlu, “The Suburban Landscape”, p. 32.

196 D. 2014, fol. 4b.

197 Necipoğlu, “The Suburban Landscape”, p. 34.

198 Thomas T. Allsen, *The Royal Hunt in Eurasian History*. Philadelphia: University of Pennsylvania Press, 2006, p. 49.

199 D. 2014, fol. 4a.

The royal hunter and his fellow heroes

Once, in 1636, we find in the garden of Davudpaşa a slightly unexpected distraction: a battue or drive (*sürgün av*).[200] This type of ring hunt, which had a long history in Eurasia, symbolised political authority and was primarily a princely venture. Technically, an encircling movement would be organised to trap masses of game. The ring would then be tightened and the animals enclosed with a fence (either ropes or nets), enabling hunters to enter and kill the game.[201] This method would normally require large areas of forest and a mass of people to do the driving. When Mehmed IV, in 1667, was on such a hunt in a forest reserve near Plovdiv/Filibe he used no less than 35,000 peasants to drive the game.[202] Mobilisations of this magnitude were of course impossible in a park. Rather, we have to imagine a number of servants hiding behind bushes and releasing the unfortunate animals, which then would be driven by a line of *ağas* and eventually massacred by the sultan and his brave boon companions.

The lack of later references to this kind of diversion might be due to the sultan's deteriorating health, which forced him to use a palanquin on his way back from the conquest of Baghdad.[203]

To hunt in the semi-private atmosphere of the royal gardens had a long tradition among Ottoman monarchs, drawing on much earlier practices.[204] Süleyman the Magnificent would even hunt in the garden of the Old Palace,[205] which stood at the site of the main buildings of today's İstanbul Üniversitesi, and Selim II is depicted on a lion hunt in Haramidere.[206] These activities in the tamed pseudo-wild landscape of

---

200 D. 525, fol. 68b.

201 Thomas T. Allsen, *The Royal Hunt*, pp. 25–29. Marc David Bear, *Honored by the Glory of Islam: Conversion and Conquest in Ottoman Europe.* New York: Oxford University Press, 2008, p. 183.

202 Bear, *Honored by the Glory of Islam*, p. 184.

203 Ziya Yılmazer, "Murad IV", *DİA* 31, Istanbul 2006, p. 182.

204 See Allsen, *The Royal Hunt*, pp. 34–51.

205 See the miniature in Hünername II. Topkapı Palace Library, H. 1525, fols. 87b–88a, published in Atasoy, *A Garden for the Sultan*, p. 231, ill. 342.

206 Mehmed b. Mehmed el-Fenari eş-şehir bi Ta'liki-zade, Şah-name veya Şema'il-name-i al-i 'Osman, Topkapı Palace Library, A. 3592, fol. 39b. Cf. Fehmi Edhem Karatay,

a royal garden, shielded from the public eye, would enhance the aura of mystery and seclusion around the ruler, which was so carefully cultivated in the course of the late 15th and the 16th centuries.[207] The inner circle of courtiers present at the spectacle would spread the rumour of these events to a wider public, and occasionally the scene would be recorded in a miniature. Yet, those sultans who really sought adventure would prefer a chase in the wild and, on horseback, could present a public spectacle of pomp and power to their subjects.[208]

Horse riding, showing off and spectacles of noble sports

Riding noble horses with precious tack was an established means of displaying status. Hence, sultans were always keen on having at their command an excellent riding stable, and Murad IV was no exception. To equip his favourite, Mustafa, in a manner befitting his exalted rank, the sultan provided him (on 3 August 1636) with golden horse trappings encrusted with emeralds and rubies, reins of sea-green silk and a gilded broad soft saddle with a golden inscription.[209] Equestrian equipment of this category would in general not have been given away without a matching horse, so we can be positive that the sultan had added a mount, even if it is not registered in a surviving document. Silahdar Mustafa did not leave his lord's lavish gift unanswered: on 14 June 1637 he paid 600 *guruş* (64,500 *akçe*)[210] for a russet (or dun) mount (*kula at*),

Topkapı Sarayı Müzesi Kütüphanesi Türkçe Yazmalar Kataloğu. II, İstanbul: Topkapı Sarayı Müzesi, 1961, p. 371, # 3030; reproduced in Filiz Çağman – Zeren Tanındı, *Topkapı Sarayı Museum Islamic Miniature Painting.* Istanbul: Tercüman, 1979, figure 56. The authors locate Haramidere in Üsküdar, but Erdoğan, "Osmanlı Devrinde İstanbul Bahçeleri", pp. 158–160, speaks of a garden bearing this name, situated between Küçükçekmece and Büyükçekmece, thus on the European shore of the Marmara Sea and its hinterland. I was not able to locate a site with this name in the area of Üsküdar.

207 See Gülru Necipoğlu, *Architecture, Ceremonial, And Power*, pp. 15–30. Cf. Allsen, *The Royal Hunt*, p. 50.

208 Cf. Allsen, *The Royal Hunt*, p. 34.

209 Göyünç, "Eski Malatya'da Silâhdar Mustafa Paşa Hanı", p. 77.

210 An unskilled labourer would have worked almost 12 years for this sum, cf. Pamuk, *İstanbul ve Diger Kentlerde 500 Yıllık Fiyatlar*, p. 70. Comparing it with an entry from

a mare, had luxurious equestrian equipment (a gold-sewn saddle pad, golden and silken trappings with tassels, and silver stirrups) brought to the garden of Istavroz by his treasurer and added a gilded silver bit in the form of a chain he himself had received as a gift by the *kadı* of Aleppo. The pasha presented all these items, together with the mare, to Murad IV in the garden of Kandilli on 27 June 1637.[211]

Noble mounts would obviously have been taken along when relocating (*göç*). Thus, when the pasha moved from Üsküdar to Tersane on 18 November 1639 he hired two 'horse boats', paying 300 *akçe* for them.[212] So one of the amusements in the gardens and beyond must have been horse riding, probably involving a display of conspicuous luxury and splendour.

Strangely enough, jereed (*cirid*), the famous old equestrian team sport, does not play any visible role in our registers, although Murad IV would have played it.[213] It seems that another physical activity, wrestling, was closer to the ruler's heart; he himself would compete from time to time in matches.[214] Moreover, Murad IV integrated wrestlers into the inner palace (*enderun*). It should be added that wrestling had a faintly religious connotation, as wrestlers had their own convents (*tekke*).[215] In December 1639, the sheikh of one of the wrestler convents received on request 5 *guruş* from Silahdar Mustafa.[216] The sultan, his favourite and other courtiers would watch wrestling matches, coddle the wrestlers with money or other gifts and reward the champions.[217] Even the highly formal banquet of Defterdarzade İbrahim Çelebi in June 1639

8 November 1639, we get an idea of the range of prices: a traveller asked the pasha to give him money for a horse and received 8 *akçe*; D. 2014, fol. 4a. Mounts were frequent gifts. Silahdar Mustafa on his way home from the conquest of Baghdad was gladdened with a horse by the *kadı* of Ankara. Another time a mount turns up among the offerings from the governor-general of Erzurum Hüseyin Pasha on 7 January 1640; ibidem, fols. 1b and 13a.

211 D. 525, fols. 12a, 84a.

212 D. 2014, fol. 4b.

213 Gökyay (ed.), *Evliya Çelebi Seyahatnâmesi.* I, pp. 104, 105.

214 Gökyay (ed.), *Evliya Çelebi Seyahatnâmesi.* I, p. 104. Yılmazer, "Murad IV", p. 182.

215 Abdülkadir Özcan, "Güreş", *DİA* 14, Istanbul 1996, p. 318.

216 D. 2014, fol. 4b.

217 D. 525, fols. 15a, 16b, 26a, 72a, 79b, 87b. D. 2014, fols. 1b, 2a.

had wrestling as one of the attractions.[218] In the end it must have been Murad's enthusiasm for this sport that gave it a prominent place in the social life of the time.

Another physical activity pursued by Silahdar Mustafa was archery. We find a number of entries referring to his presence at the Okmeydanı,[219] the shooting place of the Ottoman capital, where a number of target stones (*menzil taşı*) commemorating record-breaking shots are extant today. One championship stone, which can still be seen, celebrates a shot by Murad IV.[220] Bayezid II had an archers' convent erected there, which Silahdar Mustafa rebuilt in 1639.[221] Our register probably refers to it in a somewhat distorted but still understandable language: "At Tersane, [somebody] named Ahmed Efendi composed a chronogram and gave it to his Excellency; his Excellency gave for the convent issue a merciful gift of 10 *guruş*, on 1 Receb 1049 (28 October 1639)."[222]

Charity and involuntary and voluntary patronage of poetry

On his tours from the gardens to the palaces and elsewhere our pasha seems to have been continuously approached by various individuals asking for money. The register has a kind of general formula for these cases, naming these requests *'arz-ı hal*, "petition", which usually implies a written solicitation. As the petitioners are frequently labelled as 'poor' (*fakir*), it seems unlikely that their solicitations would have been in writing, but there is no proof. On the other hand, among the requesters were also two judges (*kadı*) asking for money, one of them jobless (*ma'zul*). He received 3 *guruş*, while his colleague was graced with 5 *guruş*.[223]

---

[218] D. 2014, fol. 2a.

[219] D. 2014, fols. 2a, 3a, 3b.

[220] Attila Bir, Mustafa Kaçar, Şinasi Acar, "Türk Menzil Okçuluğu, Yay ve Okları", *Osmanlı Bilimi Araştırmaları* VIII/ sayı 1 (2006), pp. 39–67.

[221] Filiz Gündüz, "Okmeydanı", *DİA* 33, Istanbul 2007, p. 339.

[222] D. 2014, fol. 4a: *Tersane'de Ahmed Efendi namında bir tarih söylemiş, sahib-i devlete vermişdir tekke hususı içün, in'am-ı sahib-i devlet: fi 1 Receb 1049* (28 October 1639): *guruş 10* (*'an yed-i kapucılar kethüdası*).

[223] D. 2014, fols. 4b, 5a.

Sometimes poor people would choose a more discreet way to beg money: they would bring little gifts, such as cucumbers, grapes,[224] other fruits,[225] or flowers. [226] They usually were rewarded with a sum of 2–5 *guruş* (= 240–600 *akçe*), which was not a bad deal, if we take the daily wage of an unskilled labourer to be roughly 15 *akçe.*[227] Flowers are relatively frequently mentioned, mostly carnations. They must have been very much in fashion during these years, a feature that is also found in products of art such as textiles, architectural decoration and book illumination. 'Gifts' of flowers as decent ways of begging money is already described by Busbecq.[228]

There is twice mention of someone bringing snow for cooling drinks,[229] and a number of times poets or would-be poets targeted the pasha in order to squeeze some money out of him. One poor man received 4 *guruş* for his poem, and the apparently bad rhymes of another individual yielded only 2 *guruş*, while some fairly good verses raised 10 *guruş.*[230] Better priced were *kasides* (poems of praise), fetching between 10 and 50 *guruş.*[231] An exception was the case of an Arabian dervish "uncle" (*emmi*) who sat down in Tersane, wrote a *kaside* in praise of Silahdar Mustafa, and was able to pocket only 6 *guruş.*[232] As far as I could see, none of the three poets who are mentioned by name earned any reputation in the contemporary history of Ottoman literature.

One of them was a certain Osman, who was discharged (*çıkma*) from the palace training in 1049 (1639–40),[233] but we do not know his nom de plume. Another poet, Karahisarî by name, obtained only 10 *guruş* for

---

224 D. 2014, fol. 2a.
225 D. 2014, fols. 2a, 2b, 4a.
226 D. 2014, fols. 1b, 2a, 2b.
227 Cf. Pamuk, *İstanbul ve Diger Kentlerde 500 Yıllık Fiyatlar,* p. 70.
228 Edward Seymour Forster (trsl.), *The Turkish Letters of Ogier Ghiselin de Busbecq, Imperial Ambassador at Constantinople, 1554–1562.* [2]Oxford: Oxford University Press, 1968, pp. 8–9.
229 D. 2014, fols. 2a, 3b.
230 D. 2014, fols. 2b, 3b.
231 D. 2014, fols. 4a, 5a, 9b, 14a.
232 D. 2014, fol. 4b.
233 He received on 28 Ramazan 1049 (22 January 1640) 30 *guruş* for a *kaside*. D. 2014, fol. 5a.

his *kaside*.[234] Thus, Silahdar Mustafa must not have been particularly excited by the poet.

Another poet, Tulû'î from Kalkandelen, although also not mentioned in the contemporary poets' *tezkires* (biographical dictionaries of poets), fared rather better. At least three of his works have survived the oblivion of later days: a *Pesendîdename* ("Pleasing Screed") in form of a long *kaside* dealing with Murad VI's Baghdad campaign, and a *Paşaname* ("Pasha Screed"), a rhymed *gazavatname* (heroic poem of military exploits). The latter two works have recently been studied.[235] A further *kaside* lauding Murad IV's horses[236] is a clear indication that Tulû'î was a member of the circle of artists who belonged or had access to the royal court.

Our register suggests that Tulû'î's war scenes are not accidental: he was a *çavuş* (chamberlain used as messenger) by profession[237] and must have performed this function on Murad IV's campaigns. The author himself reports that he attended one of Murad IV's soirées (*meclis*).[238] Silahdar Mustafa seems to have appreciated his poetry, giving him, on 26 October 1639, 50 *guruş* for a *kaside*.[239] The silence of the *tezkires* about Tulû'î's work is certainly due to the lacklustre quality of his poetry; while the lively narrative of events in the *Paşaname*[240] were probably the reason for the author's success at the royal court. The hero of the

234 D. 2014, fol. 5a.

235 Özer Şenödeyici – Halil Sercan Koşik, "IV. Murat'ın Bağdat Seferi Hakkında Yazılmış bir Kaside: Tulû'î'nin *Pesendîde-Nâme*'si", *Akademik Sosyal Araştırmalar Dergisi* 2, sayı 2/1 (2014), pp. 133–150. Mücahit Kaçar, "IV. Murâd Devrine Ait Manzum ve Minyatürlü bir Gazânâme: Tulûi'nin *Paşanâme* İsimli Eseri", *Türkiyat Mecmuası* 21 (2011), pp. 267–280. For a summary of the *Paşaname* see Glyn Munro Meredith-Owens, "Ken'ān Pasha's expedition against the Cossacks", *British Museum Quarterly* XXIV (1961), pp. 76–82.

236 Şenödeyici – Koşik, "IV. Murat'ın Bağdat Seferi Hakkında", p. 135.

237 On 12 Şa'ban 1049 (8 December 1639) he received one dress-length of fabric (*kumaş*) and one dress-length of *scarlatto* broadcloth for reciting a *kaside*; D. 2014, fol. 9b. The remark in Franz Babinger – [Nejat Göyünç], "Ken'ān Pasha", *Encyclopaedia of Islam*.[2] IV. Leiden 1978, p. 885, that Tulû'î was a judge is incorrect.

238 Kaçar, "IV. Murâd Devrine Ait", p. 272.

239 D. 2014, fol. 4a.

240 Cf. Kaçar, "IV. Murâd Devrine Ait", p. 277.

Paşaname is Ken'an Pasha,[241] in all likelihood Koca Ken'an Pasha, who died in 1652. The almost contemporary Sarı Ken'an Pasha (died in 1659) has also been considered to have been the model for this poetry.[242] Sarı Ken'an Pasha's career gathered pace only after Murad IV's death, when he became a boon companion of Sultan İbrahim. The expedition described in the *Paşaname* took place, however, in 1628–9,[243] which means this Ken'an Pasha must have probably belonged to the circles of Murad IV, so we can assume Koca Ken'an Pasha was meant.[244] He seems to have been in friendly contact to Silahdar Mustafa, with the latter exchanging gifts with Ken'an Pasha's sons in the summer of 1639.[245] It is also possible that this (Koca) Ken'an Pasha was married to Murad VI's sister 'Atike Sultan,[246] but as this marriage was contracted in 1633, the sons mentioned in Silahdar Mustafa's register might have come from an earlier conjugal liaison.

The trade in poetry certainly had its roots in the pasha's interest in literature and art. There is no doubt that Silahdar Mustafa was a regular guest at the colloquia of scholars (*ulema*) and sheykhs which the sultan

241 On the illustrated copy of the work in the British Library see Norah Titley, *Miniatures from Turkish Manuscripts: A Catalogue and Subject Index of Paintings in the British Library and the British Museum*. London: British Library, 1981, p. 71 # 61 and ill. 51 (Murad IV and Ken'an Pasha) and 52 (Ken'an Pasha entering Drama). Serpil Bağcı et al., *Osmanlı Resim Sanatı*. Istanbul: T.C. Kültür ve Turizm Bakanlığı Yayınları, 2006, p. 223, ill. 186 (p. 222), (Ken'an Pasha entering Drama). On the text and several miniatures of the *Paşaname* copy in London see also Tülün Değirmenci, "Sözleri Dinlensin, Tasviri İzlensin: Tulû'î'nin *Paşanâme*'si ve 17. Yüzyıldan Eşkiya Hikâyeleri", *kebikeç* 33 (2012), pp. 127–147. Three miniatures are reproduced: p. 129, Resim 1: Murad IV giving an audience; p. 134, Resim 2, Ken'an Pasha receiving a robe of honour in the sultan's presence; p. 136, Resim 3, Ken'an Pasha entering Drama.

242 Cf. Meredith-Owens, "Ken'ān Pasha's expedition", p. 77. On Sarı Ken'an Pasha see Babinger – [Göyünç], "Ken'ān Pas͟ha", pp. 884–885. Nejat Göyünyc, "Kenan Paşa", *DİA* 25, Ankara 2002, pp. 253–254.

243 Meredith-Owens, "Ken'ān Pasha's expedition", p. 77.

244 Cf. Değirmenci, "Sözleri Dinlensin, Tasviri İzlensin", p. 130, n. 9. For his career see ibidem, p. 130–131.

245 *Tersane'de Ken'an Paşa'nın oğullarından getürdi, fi 19 Rebi' I 1049* (20 July 1639)*: Hindî kutni, donluk 3; kırmızı 'Acem serid?* [= *serbend?*], *sırma uçlı, 'aded 1*, D. 2014, fol. 13a. *Tersane'de Ken'an Paşa oğullarına in'am-ı sahib-i devlet, fi 18 Rebi' II 1049* (18 August 1639)*: saye çuka, donluk 2, kumaş, donluk 4*, ibidem, fol. 9b.

246 Cf. Uluçay, *Padişahların Kadınları*, p. 52.

used to organise on Friday evenings.[247] Silahdar Mustafa's intellectual thirst is evident in our registers: as he spent 51,050 *akçe* (425.42 *guruş*) on eight books bought from Monla Çelebi of Diyarbekir,[248] perhaps the town's *kadı*; Monla Çelebi is mentioned several times in the second 'brief' register as the recipient of gifts from the pasha.[249] Alas, no book titles are given, not least because this would have gone beyond the scribe's intellectual horizon.[250] A book gift from Şa'ban Efendi, the *kadı* of Egypt, is of little help for exploring the intellectual world of Silahdar Pasha, since it was an album of calligraphies by Mir 'Emad[251] (murdered in 1615), famous for his perfecting the *nasta'lik* ductus and admired not only in Iran but also in Mughal India and the Ottoman Empire.[252] The 'long' register has an entry about a large-sized Koran, a Persian copy of Qazwīnī's famous *'Ajā'ib-i Makhlūkāt* ("Wonders of Creation") with miniatures and a *Timur-nâme* in Turkish, which the pasha handed over to his servants on 30 March 1638.[253] The latter book must have been dear to Silahdar Mustafa's heart, as he had taken it on the Baghdad campaign. It is mentioned as *tercüme-i Timur-nâme* in his campaign treasury register.[254] Thus, it cannot have been Hātifī's work by that name, as no Turkish translation is known.[255] It is more likely that Yazdī's *Zafer-name*

[247] Gökyay (ed.), *Evliya Çelebi Seyahatnâmesi.* I, p. 105. See also Nuri Özcan, "Murad IV. Mûsiki", *DİA* 31, Istanbul 2006, p. 183.

[248] D. 2014, fol 4b. For this sum an unskilled labourer would have worked more than nine years; cf. Pamuk, *İstanbul ve Diger Kentlerde 500 Yıllık Fiyatlar*, p. 70. It is probably related payments that are recorded for 10 January 1640, D. 2014, fols. 5a, 13b.

[249] D. 2014, fols. 3a, 4b, 9b.

[250] Generally the scribes of this kind of registers seem to have been poorly educated. Spelling mistakes and mishearings (obviously the texts put down were dictated) are a frequent feature.

[251] D. 2014, fol. 13a.

[252] See Kambiz Eslami, "'Emād Hasanī, Mīr, 'Emād-al-Molk", *Encyclopaedia Iranica* VIII, Costa Mesa, CA, 1998, pp. 382–385. Digital version: http://www.iranicaonline.org/articles/emad-hasani-mir (accessed 1 Oct. 2015).

[253] D. 3194, fol. 16b. For Qazwīnī's work see Günay Kut, "Acâibü'l-Mahlûkat", *DİA* I, Istanbul 1988, pp. 315–317.

[254] D. 9056, fol. 4b.

[255] I thank Birgitt Hoffmann, who brought this work to my attention. As the article by Mürsel Öztürk ("Hâtifî", *DİA* 16, Istanbul 1997, p. 468) does not mention any translation and the Türkiye Veri Taban catalogue is silent as well, it is unlikely that a translation into Turkish has ever been made.

is meant, which is extant in an Ottoman translation by Muhammed el-Buharî (Nuruosmaniye Library, no. 3268).[256]

Being the sultan's boon companion and favourite, Silahdar Mustafa might not have had sufficient leisure to read many books. He had to keep company with his lord as the sultan sailed from one garden to the next, and the time spent there was largely devoted to recreation and entertainment, with state business being a necessary evil. If we interpret records of tips and gifts, our registers contain now and again indications of the nature of the courtly group's pastimes.

Feasts, treats, fruits and luxurious flavours

Unsurprisingly, one of the favourite diversions in the gardens was feasting, although the Ottoman term for it, *ziyafet*, appears only twice in our register. In both cases the banquet was given in Tersane by people who probably did not belong to the inner circle of the royal court: one in June 1639, by Defterdarzade İbrahim Çelebi,[257] who had just been appointed finance minister of the Empire (*başdefterdar*);[258] the other banquet, a month later, hosted by the intendant of the customs (*gümrük emini*),[259] whose name, Ali Ağa, does not appear in this context but several times later, for the months of August 1639 until January 1640.[260] It is not quite clear whether these feasts took place in the gardens of the royal palace, as '*tersane*' denotes the shipyards as well as the adjacent abode of the sultan.

The seat of the admiralty not only had dockyards, boathouses and magazines but also a new *divanhane* and a small palace, the Cirid Meydanı

256 See Kaan Dilek, "Şerefeddin Ali Yezdî", *DİA* 38, Istanbul 2010, p. 551.
257 D. 2014, fol. 2a.
258 See İsmail Hâmi Danişmend, *Osmanlı Devlet Erkânı.*[2]Istanbul: Türkiye Yayınevi, 1971, p. 269 # 92. İbrahim Çelebi was the grandson of Süleyman the Magnificent's head of finances, Mustafa Çelebi.
259 D. 2014, fol. 2a.
260 D. 2014, fols. 10a, 12b, 13a, 15b.

Kasrı.[261] In the case of the customs intendant a seashore palace opposite the Tersane Palace[262] might have been the venue, as the rowers of the small boat (*permeciler*) bringing Mustafa Pasha there were tipped.[263]

The chef (*aşçıbaşı*), his team of cooks and the sultan's tasters (*çaşnigir*) repeatedly received tips and sometimes gifts of fabrics.[264] Thus, feasting must have been a frequent amusement in the gardens. The makers of sweetmeat (*şekerci, helvacı*) were somewhat less pampered.[265] Fruits, such as pears,[266] quinces,[267] lemons,[268] medlars,[269] or pomegranates,[270] brought by members of the gardeners' corps (*bostancı*) or other staff members, were certainly part of the menu, but we also come across many entries such as "graceful gift to the man who brought apples in a basket", or "to the man who brought black mulberries",[271] which point to spontaneous offerings aimed at obtaining a lavish baksheesh. In any case, Silahdar Mustafa and his companions must have consumed masses of fruits: one entry records, for November 1639, sixty baskets with fruits brought to Davudpaşa by six porters (*hamal*) and, at around the same time, another five porters were tipped for bringing fruits.[272]

In this context we should add that, according to Gelibolulu Mustafa Ali, fruits of the season were a must at drinking parties.[273] Another victual listed by the author for such events is fish, which is referred

---

261 İdris Bostan, "Tersâne-i Âmire", *DİA* 40, Istanbul 2011, p. 514.

262 D. 2014, fol. 4b.

263 D. 2014, fol. 2a.

264 D. 525, fols. 12a, 12b, 15a, 16b, 21b, 66a, 68b, 70b, 72a, 83a. The 'long' register has a list of daily wages for 12 master cooks (6–10 *akçe*) and 18 cook apprentices (5 *akçe*) and 24 established and 17 new tasters (*çaşnigir*) from the pasha (all 5 *akçe*); D. 3194, fol. 134.

265 D. 525, fols. 9b, 68b, 72a. D. 2014, fols. 2b, 3b, 4a.

266 D. 525, fol. 14b. D. 2014, fols. 2a, 4a.

267 D. 2014, fols. 3a, 3b.

268 D. 2014, fol. 1b, 2b.

269 D. 2014, fol.4a.

270 D. 2014, fol. 4b.

271 D. 525, fols. 14b, 65b.

272 D. 2014, fol. 4b.

273 Gelibolulu Mustafa Âli, *görgü ve toplum kuralları üzerinde ziyâfet sofraları (mevâidü'n-nefâis fî kavâidi'l mecâlis)*. Orhan Şaik Gökyay (ed.), Istanbul: Tercüman 1001 Temel Eser, 1978, p. 159.

to several times.[274] Sometimes these parties must have been somewhat informal. In one case, for example a flute player (*neyzen*), and not a cook, pocketed a gracious tip of 10 *guruş* for preparing a fish soup.[275] An unskilled workman would have had to work 80 days for this sum.[276] Of course, the flute player's attendance at the gathering was by no means accidental; musicians were an integral part of such events. We will come back to that issue below.

Although we know that Murad IV was a heavy and devoted drinker,[277] the registers do not contain the slightest shred of evidence of alcoholic consumption. This comes as no surprise, though. Even in the book-keeping of the royal palace kitchens and larders there are no records of wine or *rakı*, although it was definitely consumed.

Lamb, the standard meat on the menu of wealthy Ottomans, was also eaten at the banquets and parties Silahdar Mustafa gave or attended.[278] But evidently the meals were more sophisticated and exclusive than at other places. We find, for example, pickles made of grapes (*üzüm turşusu*),[279] quails (*buldırcın*)[280] and pastrami made of venison (*geyik et pastırma*).[281] A few times, confectionery made of sugar (*şeker işi*) is mentioned.[282] Such dishes, which today do not seem very special, were not part of the diet of ordinary people in pre-modern times since sugar was prohibitively expensive. The royal palace traditionally imported it from Egypt, while the sugar from Cyprus seems to have been of somewhat lower quality. Caribbean sugar imported to Europe (*Frenk şekeri*) was purchased by the royal palace for the first time in 1641.[283]

---

274 D. 2014, fol. 3b. D. 525, fol. 14b.
275 D. 2014, 3a.
276 Cf. Pamuk, *İstanbul ve Diger Kentlerde 500 Yıllık Fiyatlar*, p. 70.
277 Yılmazer, "Murad IV", p. 182.
278 D. 525, fol. 65b. D. 2014, fol. 2a.
279 D. 2014, fol. 4b.
280 D. 2014, fol. 3b.
281 D. 2014, fol. 4a.
282 D. 525, fol. 72a. D. 2014, fols. 2b, 3a, 4a.
283 Arif Bilgin, *Osmanlı Saray Mutfağı (1453–1650)*. Istanbul: Kitabevi, 2004, p. 208, n. 184. Kemalettin Kuzucu, "Tea as a New Flavour in the Ottoman Culinary Culture", Arif Bilgin – Özge Samancı (eds.), *Turkish Cuisine*. [2]Ankara: Republic of Turkey, Ministry of Culture and Tourism Publications, 2015, p. 246.

I am not going to present a list of victuals appearing in the registers, but some comestibles are so unusual or exotic that we should dwell on them for a moment. In Tersane a man brought tea (*çay*) to our pasha (26. XII. 1639),[284] which must have been still an exotic commodity at that time.[285] Contrary to the popular opinion in today's Turkey, tea did not gain currency in this country until the early years of the Republic.[286] So our register must be one of the first to mention it. The exotic character of tea was highlighted by the addition of ambergris, as two entries reveal.[287]

Ambergris (*anber*) is a substance produced in the digestive system of sperm whales. After having been oxidised for months or even years, the material acquires a fragrant smell. In earlier times it was used for perfumes and, more rarely, for adding flavour to luxurious food. It was and remains extremely expensive; in the internet I found prices as high as $ 20,000 per kilogramme.[288]

The preciousness of ambergris made it a perfect gift among members of the ruling elite. After Murad IV's death, when Silahdar Mustafa was travelling to his new post, he honoured the *kadı* and the *müftü* of Sofia and the convent of Sarı Saltuk each with a chunk of ambergris.[289]

As our *defter* indicates, Silahdar Mustafa used some of the substance for sweet fruit drinks (*şerbet*), and for *ma'cun*, a sweet paste which would either have been medicinal or taken as an aphrodisiac, depending on its ingredients. This paste was not only prepared for the pasha himself but also for Murad IV.[290] Once, in Ramazan, two handfuls of ambergris were given to cook a dish for the sultan.[291] This latter entry is, however, linguistically somewhat distorted, and the name of the dish is not given.

---

284 D. 2014, fol. 4b.

285 Cf. Bilgin, *Saray Mutfağı*, p. 211.

286 Cf. Christopher M. Hann, *Tea and the domestication of the Turkish State.* Huntingdon: Eothen Press, 1990. Kuzucu, "Tea as a New Flavour", pp. 246–247.

287 D. 2014, fol. 15b.

288 http://reprobate.co.za/ambergris-whale-doodoo-or-marine-gold/ (18 May 2015).

289 D. 2014, fol. 15b.

290 D. 2014, fol. 15b.

291 D. 2014, fol. 15b. *'Acem Rıdvan def'a sarayda Ramazan-ı şerifde hünkâr*[*a*] *pençe* (!) *pişürdiler, dirhem 10; 'an ma'rifet-i kethüda beğ iki def'a pence verilmişdir.*

Silahdar Mustafa Pasha, his high-born friend Murad IV and his privileged entourage would therefore eat exquisite food while enjoying the amenity of Ottoman garden and palace culture. The entertainment would sometimes include nocturnal fireworks, for which we find only two references, both for the summer of 1637, but without any details as to where and why the event took place.[292]

Melodies of the East

Another part of this refined mode of life was, as we have already sensed in the context of the flute player preparing fish soup, music, which had always played an important role at the Ottoman court.[293] In general, Evliya Çelebi's Book of Travels is regarded as a major source for Istanbul's music scene of the 17th century;[294] but our registers are definitely another mine of information.

Silahdar Mustafa's love for music must have been genuine. Musicians accompanied him on the march from the siege of Baghdad. When halting at Sivas the pasha rewarded his flute player (*neyzen*) Ahmed with 8 *guruş*,[295] and after Murad IV's death, when Mustafa had been removed from the capital and was travelling to his new post, the same Ahmed received in Plovdiv/Filibe one length of Parisian broadcloth.[296] Ahmed, usually termed *neyzen usta* (master flute player), was regularly spoiled by his lord with rather substantial sums.[297] The names of the musicians

[292] D. 525, fol. 14b. For fireworks see Suraiya Faroqhi, "Fireworks in Seventeenth-Century İstanbul", Öztürkmen – Vitz (eds.), *Medieval and Early Modern Performance*, pp. 181–194.

[293] Walter Denny, "Music and Musicians in Islamic Art", *Asian Music* 17/1 (1985), p. 39, speaks of music "as an essential accoutrement of royal courts in Islam".

[294] See Ersu Pekin, "Evliya Çelebi'nin müzik kaynakları", Hakan Karateke – Hatice Aynur (eds.), *Evliya Çelebi Seyahatnamesi'nin Yazılı Kaynakları*. Ankara: TTK, 2012, pp. 286–341.

[295] D. 2014, fol. 1b.

[296] D. 2014, fol 10a.

[297] D. 525, fol. 6b (20 *guruş*, probably in November or December 1636). D. 2014, fols. 3a (twice 20 *guruş* respectively in Üsküdar), 4a (10 *guruş* in Tersane, 21 October 1639, and together with six other musicians 50 *guruş* in Üsküdar, 30 October 1639), 5a

appear repeatedly, suggesting that the pasha had his own private music band. Twice a Çöğürci (choghur player) Musli is mentioned as receiving a gift of fabric in the garden of İstavroz, on 29 July 1636, and of 40 *guruş* (or 4,800 *akçe*) on 18 September 1637.[298] For 1636, a *kemanî* (violin player) Yusuf is listed among the pasha's male slaves of the *enderun* (inner palace) with a daily wage of 300 *akçe*;[299] maybe he is identical with a *zurna* player of this name who once received a gratitude of 10,000 *akçe*.[300] A trumpeter (*boruzen*) Handan was also a slave with the same pay *per diem* as Yusuf.[301] Another Yusuf, a harp player (*çengi* or *çenki*) belonged to Silahdar Mustafa's own household, as he is listed among his servants.[302] Some of Silahdar Mustafa's slaves were probably chosen because of their musical talent; they would have had music lessons and, in May 1636, a tambourine (*da'ire*) and a small violin (*kemançe*), in June a flute (*ney*), and in September another eight flutes were purchased (at 1,080 and 300 *akçe*) for them, while a year later a reed for a *zurna* was bought.[303]

It even seems that Silahdar Mustafa's connections with dervish orders were not so much religiously motivated as based in musical life. Although a number of sheikhs[304] who surface in the registers could not be identified, several entries indicate that he had good contacts with the

(5,000 *akçe* [= 41,7 *guruş*] in the pasha's palace in Istanbul, 14 February 1640), 9b (one dress-length of *scarlatto* in Tersane, 17 October 1639).

298 D. 525, fols. 15a, 70b.

299 D. 3194, fols. 128a, 129a.

300 D. 2014, fol. 5a.

301 D. 3194, fol. 128a.

302 D. 525, fol. 9b. D. 3194, fol. 129a, names him after a list of the male slaves with a daily wage of 300 *akçe*. He received once (maybe in 1637) a gratitude of 1,000 *akçe*; D. 526, fol. 9b. The entry is not dated. One Mustafa Ağa, also labelled *çengi*, received on 5 May 1637 one dress-length of heavy satin (*diba*) and one length of "fabric" (*kumaş*) in Üsküdar; ibidem, fol. 11b. In the music of Islamic lands the *çeng* (harp) normally has a female connotation; see Denny, "Music and Musicians in Islamic Art", p. 63.

303 D. 3194, fols. 34b, 35a, 36b, 40a. Whether a panpipe (*miskal*) and a *kemançe* (violin), for which 840 *akçe* were given to the Jew Nikozade, were intended for the pages (*oğlancık*) is not clear; ibidem, 36b. Nikozade seems to have taken care of a group of them, since on 8 July 1636 he received 1,500 *akçe* for the "maintenance of the little slaves"; ibidem, 36a.

304 Most prominently, Abaza Şeyh, D. 525, fols. 7a, 7b, 10b, 18a.

Mevlevi sheikhs 'Arifî and Adem Çelebi, whom he sent cash and textile gifts.[305] The Mevlevi order was particularly famous for its music.

The pasha's relations with Sheikh Ahmed Üsküdarî were more intensive; he would pamper the sheikh's man (*adamı*) regularly with money,[306] and in return receive fabrics,[307] flowers, apples, quinces and grapes from the sheikh,[308] who would be graced with imported broadcloth, Indian *kutni*,[309] Damascene *'inayet*,[310] muslin for turbans and a cashmere shawl.[311] In addition, the sheikh's son, İbrahim Ağa, once received the substantial amount of 100 *guruş*.[312] This Şeyh Ahmed Üsküdarî might be the sheikh of the Celvetiye convent in Üsküdar,[313] founded by Aziz Mahmud Hüdayi as a branch of the Bayramiye and related to the Halvetiye order.[314] As the convents of the Celvetiye in Üsküdar were centres of musical life,[315] Silahdar Mustafa's ties with this order might have been based on music as well.

All this does not mean that the pasha was irreligious. Silahdar Mustafa would regularly reward converts to Islam with sums of between 10 and 25 *guruş*,[316] or with garments.[317] He would give financial support

305 D. 2014, fols. 2b, 4b, 9b, 15b.
306 D. 525, fols. 15a, 66a.
307 D. 525, fol. 73b.
308 D. 2014, fols. 2b, 4a.
309 *Kutni* or *Kutnu* was a thick fabric woven mostly with a warp of silk and a weft of cotton (or flax) or a mixture of cotton and silk; Hülya Tezcan, *Atlaslar Atlası: Pamuklu, Yün ve İpek Kumaş Koleksiyonu/Cotton, Woolen and Silk Fabrics Collection*. Istanbul: YKY, 1993, p. 28.
310 Damascene (Şam) *'inayet* is listed among silks and *kutnis* in the register of officially fixed prices from 1640; Mübahat S. Kütükoğlu, *Osmanlılarda Narh Müessesesi ve 1640 Tarihli Narh Defteri*. Istanbul: Enderun Kitabevi, 1983, p. 116.
311 D. 2014, fol. 9b.
312 D. 2014, fol. 2a.
313 Cf. H. Kâmil Yılmaz, *Azîz Mahmûd Hüdâyî ve Celvetiyye Tarîkatı*. Istanbul: ERKAM, 1999, pp. 131–132. I am grateful to Kemal Beydilli and Davut Erkan, Istanbul, who provided me with this reference.
314 See Hasan Kâmil Yılmaz, "Celvetiyye", *DİA* 7, Istanbul 1993, pp. 273–275.
315 Yılmaz, "Celvetiyye", p. 275.
316 D. 2014, fols. 1b, 3a, 4a, 4b, 5a.
317 When the head carpenter of a maona converted on the occasion of the ship's launch, he received on 10 January 1640 a turban and a turban muslin; D. 2015, fol 10a. Two (captured ?) Spaniards (? *Sipan*) coming from Nova (today Herceg Novi) who converted to Islam on 16 May 1636 were rewarded with a dress-length of *atlas* (light

to pilgrims going to Mecca, such as the *imam* of the Süleymaniye mosque and others,[318] and, on 4 November 1639, he sent the substantial sum of 208 gold pieces with the *surre* (the annual gift dispatch to Mecca) to the Holy Sites.[319] In October 1636 he bought a diamond framed by other precious stones which was sent to Medina.[320] Moreover, he seems to have included in his endowment of the *han* in Malatya a portion for Mecca and Medina; at least an entry referring to "his mosque sweeper" (*ferraş*), a sheikh in Medina,[321] suggests such an arrangement. Furthermore, the pasha would repeatedly buy Koran copies,[322] which might, however, have been intended as gifts to other officials. He took care of the religiously proper conduct of his slaves by purchasing two little boys to act as their *muezzins*.[323]

Murad IV, who was a gifted composer himself, reinvigorated musical life at court and made it flourish again. From Tabriz, which he took in 1635, he brought twelve musicians to Istanbul, the most famous of them being Şeştârî Murad Ağa.[324] In our register he appears as *tanburî* Hass Murad.[325] There is little doubt that *tanburî* Hass Murad and Şeştârî Murad are one and the same person, since a *şeştâr* is a six-stringed lute, while *tambur* is a more general term for a lute. The Persian influence on the musical performance must have been considerable. One blind Persian singer named Ahmed and another 'Persian' (*'Acem*) blind singer

satin) each. Hence they must have come from an elevated background; either they had been officers or aristocrats. The status of a converting individual was usually maintained by the Ottoman authorities; cf. Hedda Reindl-Kiel, "Das Ende einer Kavaliersreise – Beginn einer osmanischen Karriere?", eadem – Seyfi Kenan (eds.), *Deutsch-türkische Begegnungen/Alman Türk Tesadüfleri. Festschrift für Kemal Beydilli/Kemal Beydilli'ye Armağan.* Berlin: EB-Verlag, 2013, pp. 138–139.

318 D. 2014, fols. 3a, 4a.

319 D. 2014, fol. 13a.

320 D. 3194, fols. 36b, 37b.

321 D. 2014, fol. 1b.

322 D. 3194, fol. 34b, 35a, 39b.

323 D. 3194, fol. 39a.

324 Nuri Özcan, "Murad Ağa, Şeştârî", *DİA* 32, Istanbul 2006, p. 185. İsmail Hakkı Uzunçarşılı, "Osmanlılar Zamanında Saraylarda Musiki Hayatı", *Belleten* XLI/161 (1977), p. 90.

325 D. 2014, fols. 2a, 3a, 4a, 9b.

Mahmud repeatedly received rewards.[326] Several times a blind Persian singer is mentioned, without giving his name, so we do not know, whether Ahmed, Mahmud or a third person is meant.[327] Another Persian singer and lute player, Rıdvan, worked as a pickles maker and confectioner in Silahdar Mustafa's household, preparing sophisticated pickles, splendid *şerbets* and extravagantly flavoured sweets.[328] The relatively large group of musicians of Iranian origin employed by the sultan and his favourite friend hint at a rather Persianate taste in music and a preference for melodies of the East.

The musicians in Silahdar Mustafa's service were multinational: a certain Cüfut Hasan Ağa,[329] as his byname suggests probably of Jewish descent, and an Albanian singer, Mehmed,[330] a member of the pasha's guard of honour,[331] figure most prominently in the records. Cüfut Hasan in all likelihood did not originally belong to Silahdar Mustafa's staff of servants. For, in June 1639, he obtained 30 *guruş* for shaving his beard (*sakal*).[332] Wearing a beard was a status symbol that would not have been conceded to servants of low standing.[333] Did the shaving ceremony mark Cüfut Hasan's integration into the pasha's household? If so, he must have belonged to the higher ranking staff. The relatively substantial rewards and gifts do point in this direction. Once, apparently after a performance in the palace of Üsküdar, he is named with his fellow singers and bears the title *çelebi* (at that time interchangeable with *ağa*).[334] This again is an indication of some status. It seems that he was employed in Silahdar Mustafa's finance administration, since he is mentioned as purchasing musk at the behest of his lord.[335] Indeed, he must have had a number of

---

326 D. 2014, fols. 2a, 2b, 3a, 3b, 4a, 9b, 10b.
327 D. 2024, fols. 2b, 3a, 10b, 13b.
328 D. 2014, fols. 2b, 4a, 4b, 15b.
329 D. 525, fols.15a, 26a, 65b, 70a, 82b. D. 2014, fols. 2a, 3a, 9b,
330 D. 525, fols. 6b, 10b. D. 2014, fols. 2a, 4a, 16a.
331 D. 525, fol. 10b, 65b (?).
332 D. 2014, fol. 2a.
333 d'Ohsson, *Tableau général,* VI/1, p. 128.
334 D. 2014, fol. 4a.
335 D. 2014, fol. 5a.

talents, since Evliya Çelebi calls him an 'imitator' (*mukallid*),[336] which was an old established character in courtly amusements.[337]

One gets the impression that Mustafa Pasha would pick up musicians wherever he could find them. When, according to an entry for 29 August 1639, he went to the "dungeon of the flute players" at Tersane, he gave 12 *guruş* to those imprisoned flute players who were ill. On the same occasion two flautists standing by the wayside received 2 *guruş* because they were sick.[338]

The term "dungeon of the flute players" is rather odd, since a facility of this name is completely unknown. Yet, the Maritime Arsenal did have a jail where the galley slaves (prisoners of war and convicted criminals) were kept, the notorious *Bagno*, which included an infirmary, named al Santo Paolo.[339] The record might well refer to this prison. Does this mean that Mustafa Pasha had formed a music band of galley slaves? In any case, he was willing to improve the living conditions in this place of misery by having pipes laid there to supply water.[340]

In June 1639 a French physician – possibly consulted for the sultan's illness – introduced a new musician, unfortunately nothing is said about the latter's name or nationality.[341]

It was also a physician, Master (*usta*) Mehmed from Kasımpaşa, who sent in September 1639 the singer (*hanende*) Kasımpaşalı Osman Çelebi,[342] who seems to have been (or become) a well-known musi-

336 Gökyay (ed.), *Evliya Çelebi Seyahatnâmesi.* I, p. 105.

337 Cf. Özdemir Nutku, "Clowns at Ottoman Festivals", Öztürkmen – Vitz (eds.), *Medieval and Early Modern Performance*, p. 201.

338 D. 2014, fol. 3a. The door keepers of the prison and guards (*vardiyan*) of ships were included in the pasha's benevolence, each receiving 11 *guruş* (ibidem). The *vardiyans* were a navy unit (*bölük*) who had the task of guarding their ship and of communicating the orders of the ship's captain to the crew; see İdris Bostan, *Osmanlı Bahriye Teşkilâtı: XVII. Yüzyılda Tersâne-i Âmire.* Ankara: TTK, 1992, p. 56.

339 Müller-Wiener, "Zur Geschichte des Tersâne-i Âmire in Istanbul", p. 257.

340 D. 2014, fol. 4a (the pipelayer Hass Osman received 86 *guruş* for expenses related to the planned water supply for the dungeon, 17 October 1639).

341 D. 2014, fol. 2a.

342 D. 2014, fol. 3b.

cian[343] and is mentioned a number of times in our register.[344] Silahdar Mustafa once even paid 3,700 *akçe* and at another time 5,000 *akçe* for the construction of a dwelling (*oda*) for him in Üsküdar.[345] Several musicians were residents of Istanbul, such as a lute player (*barbûtî*) Ahmed from Beşiktaş.[346] And a whole group from Kasımpaşa struck up on one occasion.[347]

Wine, women and song – without women...

When we speak about courtly music we tend to imagine a dignified, grave and solemn scene, very much in the style as in the miniature described above. But the music set the mood not only for exquisite food and moderate enjoyment of wine but – at least sometimes – for the Ottoman version of wine, women and song, albeit mostly without females, who would be substituted by *çengis*, young male dancers dressed up as women.[348] Evliya Çelebi gives a whole list of these dancers and other night owls who came from the "seventy cells of the bastards" (*veled-i zinanın yetmiş çilelerinden*). With such a group of dancers, revellers and *şehir oğlanları* ("city boys")[349] Murad IV would push the boat out on

343 Nuri Özcan, "Murad IV. Mûsiki", *DİA* 31, p. 183. Gökyay (ed.), *Evliya Çelebi Seyahatnâmesi.* I, p. 302.

344 D. 2014, fols. 3a, 3b, 4a, 5a, 16a.

345 D. 2014, fol. 3a.

346 D. 2014, fol. 4a. He might be identical with the *tanburî* Beşiktaşlı Merzevîr (?) Ahmed; ibidem, fol. 2a.

347 Listed are *tanburî* Murad, Behram and an unnamed panpipe player (*miskalcı*), D. 2014, fol. 3a.

348 The term *çengi* is today understood as female dancer, but in Ottoman times it was used for dancing boys and girls, see Metin And, *A Pictorial History of Turkish Dancing from folk dancing to whirling dervishes – belly dancing to ballet.* Ankara: Dost Yayınları, 1976, p. 138. The whole setting revealed in our documents makes it more than unlikely that girls were meant.

349 Walter G. Andrews – Mehmet Kalpaklı, *The Age of Beloveds. Love and the Beloved in Early-Modern Ottoman and European Culture and Society.* [2]Durham – London: Duke University Press, 2006, p. 42, explains *şehir oğlanları* as "a palace term for young, urban, nonslave nonelites".

Monday nights until the early morning. Evliya labels this kind of parties fancifully *Hüseyin Baykara meclisleri.*[350]

The dancers were, it seems, procured by a professional impresario, a *çengici*, who might have also provided a violin player (*kemençe*) and one of the town's young male beauties (*şehir oğlanı*)[351] of the kind praised in the *şehrengiz* literature.[352] In 1636 Silahdar Mustafa had a kaftan of yellow *darayı* tailor-made for an unnamed 'city boy'.[353] This must have been the İbrahim who is listed, with the explanatory note *şehir oğlanı*, among Silahdar Mustafa's male slaves (*gılman*) of the inner palace (*enderun*) as receiving a daily wage of 300 *akçe*.[354] Tülün Değirmenci has demonstrated that these boys were in miniatures often depicted with a book;[355] thus, they must have been essential figures at literary parties. In July 1639, a banquet given by Ali Ağa, the intendant of the customs (*gümrük emini*) deployed musicians, *çengis* and someone called Kara Ceylan, "the black gazelle",[356] presumably again a young male beauty.

This homoerotic atmosphere should not lead us, however, to false conclusions.[357] We have already mentioned that Silahdar Mustafa obvi-

350 Gökyay (ed.), *Evliya Çelebi Seyahatnâmesi.* I, p. 105. Husayn Baykara was the Timurid ruler of Khorasan (1469–1506), see Hans R. Roemer, "Hosayn Bāyqarā", *Encyclopaedia Iranica* XII, New York, N. Y. 2004, pp. 508–5011. Digitalised version: http://www.iranicaonline.org/articles/hosayn-bayqara (accessed: 10 October 2015). For the *mecalis* (sophisticated parties) of Husayn Baykara see Thomas W. Lentz – Glenn D. Lowry, *Timur and the Princely Vision: Persian Art and Culture in the Fifteenth Century.* (Exhibition Catalogue) Los Angeles: County Museum of Art – Washington: Arthur M. Sackler Gallery, Smithsonian Institution Press, 1989, pp. 257–259.

351 D. 525, fol. 15a.

352 This is a particularly Ottoman form of poetry praising the physical and human beauties of a town. Many of the human beauties were male adolescents attached to a craft. See Agâh Sırrı Levend, *Türk Edebiyatında Şehr-engizler ve Şehr-engizlerde İstanbul.* Istanbul: Baha, 1958. See also Tülün Değirmenci, "Osmanlı Tasvir Sanatında Görselin "Okuması": İmgenin Ardındaki Hikâyeler (Şehir Oğlanları ve İstanbul'un Meşhur Kadınları)", *Osmanlı Araştırmaları/The Journal of Ottoman Studies* 45 (2015), pp. 29–38.

353 D. 3194, fol. 50a. *Darayı* is a light silk, related to taffeta, see Fahri Dalsar, *Türk Sanayi ve Ticaret Tarihinde Bursa'da İpekçilik.* İstanbul: Sermet Matbaası, 1960, p. 57.

354 This sum was also paid to the other slaves mentioned in the list; only a few senior slaves received 360 *akçe* per day; D. 3194, fol. 129.

355 Değirmenci, "Osmanlı Tasvir Sanatında", pp. 29–30.

356 D. 2014, fol. 2a.

357 For this topic cf. Andrews – Kalpaklı, *The Age of Beloveds*, pp. 11–18.

ously had a *harem*. Furthermore, although Murad IV did not leave a male heir when he died in 1640, at the age of just 28 he had fathered no less than 16 children.[358]

At least once a woman was present at a late night party in the garden of Hasan Kalfa in Arnavudköy: a lady masqueraded as an old, wrinkled woman came from the sultan (who apparently had sent her).[359] The party guests must have considered this tremendous fun, and the lady received a full purse of *çil akçe*. Even though such buffoonery seems somewhat childish to us, we must not forget it was the strict separation of genders that triggered silly games of this kind. Almost a century later, allegedly men, presided over by grand vizier Damad İbrahim Pasha, would flip gold coins at the veil of ladies and find this a proper way of merrymaking.[360]

Campaigns, ships, dockyards and a reliable deputy

Although at first glance our registers seem to represent a garland of amusements, festivities, friendships and precious or simple gifts passing to and fro, the entries contain a range of indications of more serious activity. The first register has several references to the march against Baghdad, the siege and the Ottoman triumph,[361] but almost nothing about Silahdar Mustafa Pasha's official actions. Whether two dozen (*deste*) of red paper sheets, brought to the pasha by his treasurer on 22 August 1636 in Üsküdar,[362] were linked to Silahdar Mustafa's duties is questionable. We find the purchase of lances (*mızrak*) 'for the ruler' costing 14,350 *akçe* on 31 July 1636 and of gunpowder for 800 *akçe* on

358 Yılmazer, "Murad IV", p. 182.
359 D. 2014, fol. 1b.
360 Madline Zilfi, "Women and Society in the Tulip Era, 1718–1730", Amira El Azhari Sonbol (ed.), *Women, the Family and Divorce: Laws in Islamic History*. Syracuse, N.Y.: Syracuse University Press, 1996, p. 293.
361 D. 525, fols. 6a, 32b.
362 D. 525, fol. 72b.

2 August 1637.[363] As preparation for the campaign against Baghdad on 18 March 1638 one dress-length of fabric (probably *atlas*, light satin) was turned into envelopes for letters.[364] On another occasion, this time for letters or orders written during the various trips and sojourns in the gardens of Istanbul and its environs, a dress-length of fabric was used for the same purpose.[365]

As already mentioned, the second register records a number of stops made on the way back from Baghdad, from Diyarbakır onward.[366] Furthermore, this *defter* contains quite a lot of information about the pasha's activity as admiral of the fleet. On the march back to the Ottoman capital he was already having to deal with official documents. In Zile, for instance, he received a letter from Maksud Ağa, the *emin* (intendant) of the Maritime Arsenal,[367] who handled financial matters and supervised the construction and repair of ships, their equipment and manning.[368] It informed the new admiral that 32 new ships had set sails for the Black Sea and two for the Mediterranean, described the situation of the fleet in both seas and provided the latest intelligence.[369] The register indicates that our pasha was corresponding with Algiers,[370] with the governor-general of Tripolis (in today's Lebanon),[371] with Salonica[372] and with Chios.[373]

---

363 D. 525, fols. 14b and 12b.

364 D. 525, fol. 20b.

365 D. 525, fol. 83a (no date).

366 D. 2014, fol. 1b.

367 D. 2024, fol. 1b. The entry is not dated; but Maksud Ağa's original letter is preserved in the archives of the Topkapı Palace and bears a note on the verso: "On 21 Muharrem in the year 1049 (24 May 1639) [this letter] arrived at the *menzil* of Zile from Istanbul from Maksud Efendi." Victor Ostapchuk, "Five Documents from the Topkapı Palace Archive on the Ottoman Defense of the Black Sea against the Cossacks (1639)", Bernard Lewis et al. (eds.), *Raiyyet Rüsûmu: Essays presented to Halil İnalcık on his Seventieth Birthday by his Colleagues and Students.* = *Journal of Turkish Studies* 11 (1987). p. 70.

368 İsmail Hakkı Uzunçarşılı, *Osmanlı Devletinin Merkez ve Bahriye Teşkilâtı.* [2]Ankara 1984, pp. 425–426. Ostapchuk, "Five Documents", p. 52, n. 11.

369 Ostapchuk, "Five Documents", pp. 69–75.

370 D. 2014, fol. 4b.

371 D. 2014, fol. 4b.

372 D. 2014, fol. 4a.

373 D. 2014, fol. 2b.

So although Silahdar Mustafa had no naval experience, he evidently administered and supervised the matters of the Ottoman fleet from the Ottoman capital, while leaving implementation on the spot to the vice-admiral (*tersane kethüdası*) Piyale and his men.

We learn that a number of new ships, a *baştarda*[374] (smaller war galley, used by top level navy commanders[375]), a maona[376] (war galley with 26 thwarts[377]), a ship of an unspecified type named the Haguna[378] and a sailing ship, called the Pajdariye[379] were built and launched. Another unspecified older ship, the Bâjdâr is mentioned because her senior guards (*vardiyanbaşı*) were kept happy with a gift of 40 *guruş* on 21 June 1639.[380] During the 16th and more or less the first half of the 17th centuries, the Ottoman admiralty preferred, according to İdris Bostan, galley-type warships.[381] So was the Pajdariye a first attempt to return to sailing vessels?

Before the launch of a new ship the chief astrologer (*müneccimbaşı*) Hasan Çelebi would be consulted and a ceremony held, accompanied by military music and the sultan's gift of a robe of honour to the admiral.[382] The pasha would regularly inspect the seaworthiness of the *kadırgas* (galleys)[383] and the maonas by ordering them to sail around.[384] On these

---

374 D. 2014, fol. 5a.

375 See İdris Bostan, *Kürekli ve Yelkenli Osmanlı Gemileri*. Istanbul: Bilge, 2005, pp. 172–188.

376 D. 2014, fol. 10a.

377 The vessel was 49 m long, wider and higher than a *baştarda* and had two or three masts; Bostan, *Kürekli ve Yelkenli*, pp. 221–224.

378 D. 2014, fol. 1b.

379 D. 2014, fol. 10a, 13b. The *Pajdariye* was launched on 14 January 1640; as the sailors (*yelkenci*) and the captain were awarded at this occasion with two dress-lengths (*donluk*) of purple (*mor*) broadcloth and four pieces of ordinary turban muslin, the ship must have been a sailing vessel.

380 D. 2014, fol. 2a.

381 Bostan, *Kürekli ve Yelkenli*, p. 269.

382 D. 2014, fols. 5a, 10a, 13a, 13b. For the ceremony in later times see Tuncay Zorlu, "Ottoman Ship Launching Ceremonies: A Practise between Symbols and Rites", *International Review of Turkology* I (2008), pp. 55–64.

383 A *kadırga* had 25 thwarts and 196 (or up to 245) oarsmen and was at that time 41,5 m (or 42,5 m) long; Bostan, *Kürekli ve Yelkenli*, pp. 192 and 198.

384 D. 2014, fols. 2b, 3b, 4a, 4b, 5a.

occasions he would also have the coal bunkers and powder magazines checked.[385]

Silahdar Mustafa must have regularly visited and inspected the dockyard and arsenal of Tersane on the Golden Horn, although we have only one reference for such an inspection tour.[386] The staff of the dockyards tried to make the admiral's tours enjoyable. For instance, the *kethüda* (vice admiral) of the docks, Uzun Piyale, once sent a 'Frank' carrying a monkey.[387]

Piyale, an experienced captain,[388] was the right man in the right place. While holding the official rank of vice admiral, he also functioned time and again as Silahdar Mustafa's proxy. He travelled to places such as Chios[389] and had command over the Ottoman naval forces in the Black Sea. He was to defend the Ottoman fort of Özü (Ochkiv, Russ. Ochakov) and to fight against the Cossacks at the important fortress at the mouth of the river Don, Azak (Azov), which had fallen into their hands in 1637.[390] The relationship between him and Silahdar Mustafa seems to have been cordial since, in January 1640, the *kethüda* presented his lord with underwear and linen as a gift for the Sugar Feast.[391] The gifting of underwear was generally an indication of sincere friendship.[392]

385 D. 2014, fol. 4b.
386 D. 2014, fol. 3b.
387 D. 2014, fol. 4b.
388 Cf. Victor Ostapchuk, "Five Documents", pp. 51, 64–68, 86–101.
389 D. 2014, fol. 2b.
390 *'Abdülkādir Efendi Tarihi* II, p. 117. Göyünç, "Eski Malatya'da Silâhdar Mustafa Paşa Hanı", p. 72. Ostapchuk, "Five Documents", *passim*.
391 D. 2014, fol. 12b.
392 The most prominent example of such a gift is the dispatch of two sets of underwear for the Polish king Sigismund II Augustus (1520–1572) by Süleyman the Magnifent's beloved consort Hürrem (Roxelana, approx. 1500–1558); Uğur Ünal and Władysław Stępniak (eds.), *Yoldaki Elçi: Osmanlı'dan Günümüze Türk-Leh İlişkileri / Poseł w drodze: Stosunki turecko – polskie od czasów osmańskich do dnia dzisiejszego*. Istanbul: T.C. Başbakanlık Devlet Arşivleri Genel Müdürlüğü, 2014, pp. 36–37.

In lieu of a conclusion: the question of an Ottoman leisure class

Even when the registers refer to items or actions connected with the pasha's official duties they leave us with an impression of ease and leisure. Yet, we must not forget that even book-keeping records have bias. For they certainly reflect the viewpoint of a somewhat simple-minded and semi-educated scribe for whom the pasha's doings might often have appeared random and rather frivolous. To gain a more balanced picture, we should bear in mind the pasha's many obligations and responsibilities. Even then, however, a good part of the records does point to a relatively leisurely life, even if an appropriate term or concept had not yet been formulated to express it.

The literature does not speak of a leisure class when referring to the wealthy upper echelons of Ottoman society, but of a "ruling elite". When doing so, we target not only to the very small circle of politicians governing the empire but also the potential candidates for the highest ranks of the state and their social milieu. In a way we use the term to avoid expressions such as aristocracy. Indeed, leaving aside families such as the Evrenosoğlus, the Mihaloğlus, the Malkoçoğlus and a few *'ulema* (scholar) families, the Ottoman Empire had virtually no blood aristocracy up to the 18th century, when the process of transforming the *'ayan* (notable) class was completed. In fact, at least from the 15th century onwards in the Ottoman Empire, and in modern Turkey until this very day, we witness the emergence of a new 'ruling elite' once every century.

In the second half of the 15th and during the 16th century the leading group consisted largely of men from the Balkans who made their way to the royal palace via the *devşirme,* often dramatically called 'blood tax', and of other converts to Islam. The seventeenth century is seen as the time of the great households, as many leading figures did not start their career in the royal court but had their training in the large pasha households.[393] And, in the early 17th century, we again see another feature so far scarcely noticed in the literature: members of the wealthy bourgeoisie managed to get an education for their sons in the royal palace – Evliya Çelebi being a good example – and enabled a number of these boys to make a career in the state administration, while others, such as Evliya, pursued their hobbies or led a leisurely life. So, in this context, the question arises as to whether we can see here the emergence of an – albeit very small – 'leisure class' in a sense close to Thorstein Veblen's use, even if such a class was to remain in its infancy.

The two registers we have explored proved to be a mine of information about daily life and daily pleasure in the courtly society of the late years of Murad IV. Whether this life style would and could have been shared – at least to a certain degree, even if at a lower level – by members of an emergent grand bourgeoisie remains unclear. But the later fate of Silahdar Mustafa is a vivid illustration of why such a social group never gained prominence in the Ottoman system. Wealth was generally equated with power and therefore only tolerated as long as an individual stayed in office or could be needed for future tasks. A fortune that became too large could be perilous for its owner, who would often pay with his life. One reason for the longevity of the Ottoman dynasty lay certainly in this mechanism.

---

393 Cf. Rifa'at Abou-el-Haj, "The Ottoman Vezir-Pasha Households 1683–1703: A preliminary report", *Journal of the American Oriental Society* 94/4 (1974), pp. 438–447.

Bibliography

Primary Sources

Başbakanlık Osmanlı Arşivi:

Maliyeden Müdevver (MAD) 6067.

Maliyeden Müdevver (MAD) 14724.

Topkapı Sarayı Müzesi Arşivi:

D. 525.

D. 2014.

D. 3194.

D. 9056.

D. 9575.

D. 10034.

D. 10535.

Narratives:

'Abdülkādir Efendi: *Topçular Kâtibi 'Abdülkādir (Kadrî) Efendi Tarihi.* (Metin ve Tahlîl) II. Ziya Yılmazer (ed.), Ankara: TTK, 2003.

Atsız, Buğra: *Das Osmanische Reich um die Mitte des 17. Jahrhunderts. Nach den Chroniken des Vecihi (1637–1660) und des Mehmed Halifa (1633–1660).* München: Dr. Dr. Rudolf Trofenik, 1977.

Ayvansarayî, Hafız Hüseyin: *Hadikat al-Cevami.* II. Istanbul: Matba'a-ı 'amire, 1281 (1864–5).

Crane, Howard (trsl.): *The Garden of the Mosques: Hafız Hüseyin al-Ayvansarayî's Guide to the Muslim Monuments of Ottoman Istanbul.* Leiden etc.: Brill, 2000.

Dankoff, Robert (trsl.): *The Intimate Life of an Ottoman Statesman: Melek Ahmed Pasha (1588–1662) as portrayed in Evliya Çelebi's Book of Travels (Seyahat-name).* Albany, N.Y.: SUNY, 1991.

Forster, Edward Seymour (trsl.): *The Turkish Letters of Ogier Ghiselin de Busbecq, Imperial Ambassador at Constantinople, 1554–1562.* ²Oxford: Oxford University Press, 1968.

Fresne-Canaye, Philippe du: *Le Voyage du Levant.* M. H. Hauser (ed.), Paris: Ernest Leroux, 1897. Reprint: Frankfurt/Main: Institute for the History of Arabic-Islamic Science, 1995.

Gelibolulu Mustafa Âli: *görgü ve toplum kuralları üzerinde ziyâfet sofraları (mevâidü'n-nefâis fî kavâidi'l mecâlis).* Orhan Şaik Gökyay (ed.), Istanbul: Tercüman 1001 Temel Eser, 1978.

Gökyay, Orhan Şaik (ed.): *Evliya Çelebi Seyahatnâmesi. Evliya Çelebi b. Derviş Muhammed Zıllî.* 1. Kitap: İstanbul. Istanbul: YKB, 1996.

Kreutel, Richard F.: *Kara Mustafa vor Wien: 1683 aus der Sicht türkischer Quellen.* Karl Teply (ed.), Graz-Wien-Köln: Styria, 1982.

Kütükoğlu, Mübahat S.: *Osmanlılarda Narh Müessesesi ve 1640 Tarihli Narh Defteri.* Istanbul: Enderun Kitabevi, 1983.

Naîmâ Mustafa Efendi: *Târih-i Na'îmâ (Ravzatü 'l-Hüseyn fî Hulâsati Ahbâri 'l-Hâfikayn).* 4 vols. Mehmet İpşirli (ed.), Ankara: TKK, 2007.

Ohsson, [Ignatius] M[ouradgea] d': *Tableau général de l'empire Othoman, divisé en deux parties, dont l'une comprend la Législation Mahométane; l'autre, L'Histoire de l'Empire Othoman.* VI/1, Paris: imprimerie de monsieur [Firmin Didot] 1791.

Peçevî İbrahim Efendi: *Tarîh-i Peçevî.* Fahri Ç. Derin and Vahit Çabuk (eds.), Istanbul: Enderun Kitabevi, 1980.

Ricaut, Sir Paul: *History of the Present State of the Ottoman Empire.* [3]London: R. Clavell, J. Robinson and A. Churchill, 1686.

Schmid zum Schwarzenhorn, Johann Rudolf: "Finalrelation Nr. 1", ed. Peter Meienberger, *Johann Rudolf Schmid zum Schwarzenhorn als kaiserlicher Resident in Konstantinopel in den Jahren 1629–1643. Ein Beitrag zur Geschichte der diplomatischen Beziehungen zwischen Österreich und der Türkei in der ersten Hälfte des 17. Jahrhunderts.* Bern: Herbert Lang, – Frankfurt/M.: Peter Lang, 1973, pp. 159–190.

Schweigger, Salomon: *Ein newe Reyßbeschreibung auß Teutschland Nach Constantinopel und Jerusalem.* Nürnberg: Johann Lantzenberger, 1608. Reprint: Graz: Akademische Druck- u. Verlagsanstalt, 1964.

Ünal, Uğur – Władysław Stępniak (eds.): *Yoldaki Elçi: Osmanlı'dan Günümüze Türk-Leh İlişkileri / Poseł w drodze: Stosunki turecko – polskie od czasów osmańskich do dnia dzisiejszego.* Istanbul: T.C. Başbakanlık Devlet Arşivleri Genel Müdürlüğü, 2014.

Secondary Sources

Abou-el-Haj, Rifaʿat: "The Ottoman Vezir-Pasha Households 1683–1703: A preliminary report", *Journal of the American Oriental Society* 94/4 (1974), pp. 438–447.

Allsen, Thomas T: *The Royal Hunt in Eurasian History.* Philadelphia: University of Pennsylvania Press, 2006.

And, Metin: *A Pictorial History of Turkish Dancing from folk dancing to whirling dervishes – belly dancing to ballet.* Ankara: Dost Yayınları, 1976.

Andrews, Walter G.– Mehmet Kalpaklı: *The Age of Beloveds. Love and the Beloved in Early-Modern Ottoman and European Culture and Society.* [2]Durham – London: Duke University Press, 2006.

Artan, Tülay: "Davutpaşa Bahçesi", *Dünden Bugüne İstanbul Ansiklopedisi.* III. Istanbul: Kültür Bakanlığı/Tarih Vakfı, 1994, pp. 10–11.

Artan, Tülay: "Fener Bahçesi", *Dünden Bugüne İstanbul Ansiklopedisi.* III, Istanbul: Kültür Bakanlığı/Tarih Vakfı, 1994, pp. 281–282.

Artan, Tülay: "Fener Köşkü", *Dünden Bugüne İstanbul Ansiklopedisi.* III, Istanbul: Kültür Bakanlığı/Tarih Vakfı, 1994, pp. 282–283.

Artan, Tülay– Christoph K. Neumann: "Kavak Sarayı", *Dünden Bugüne İstanbul Ansiklopedisi.* IV, Istanbul: Kültür Bakanlığı/Tarih Vakfı, 1994, pp. 494–495.

Atasoy, Nurhan: *A Garden for the Sultan: Gardens and flowers in the Ottoman culture.* [Istanbul]: Aygaz, 2002.

Atasoy, Nurhan: *Otağ-ı Hümayun: Osmanlı Çadırları.* Istanbul: Aygaz, 2000.

Ayan, Hüseyin (ed.): *Cevrî: Hayâtı, Edebî Kişiliği, Eserleri ve Divanının Tenkidli Metni.* Erzurum 1981.

Ayan, Hüseyin: "Cevrî İbrahim Çelebi", *Türkiye Diyanet Vakfı İslâm Ansiklopedisi.* 7, Istanbul 1993, pp. 460–461.

Babinger, Franz – [Nejat Göyünç]: "Kenʿān Pasha", *Encyclopaedia of Islam.*[2] IV. Leiden 1978, pp. 884–885.

Bağcı, Serpil – Filiz Çağman – Günsel Renda – Zeren Tanındı: *Osmanlı Resim Sanatı.* Istanbul: T.C. Kültür ve Turizm Bakanlığı Yayınları, 2006.

Bear, Marc David: *Honored by the Glory of Islam: Conversion and Conquest in Ottoman Europe.* New York: Oxford University Press, 2008.

Bilgin, Arif: *Osmanlı Saray Mutfağı (1453–1650).* Istanbul: Kitabevi, 2004.

Bir, Attila – Mustafa Kaçar – Şinasi Acar: "Türk Menzil Okçuluğu, Yay ve Okları", *Osmanlı Bilimi Araştırmaları* VIII/ sayı 1 (2006), pp. 39–67.

Borschberg, Peter: "The Euro-Asian Trade in Bezoar Stones (approx. 1500 to 1700)", Michael North (ed.), *Artistic and Cultural Exchanges between Europe and Asia, 1400–1900.* Franham, Surrey: Ashgate, 2010, pp. 29–43.

Bostan, İdris: *Kürekli ve Yelkenli Osmanlı Gemileri.* Istanbul: Bilge, 2005.

Bostan, İdris: *Osmanlı Bahriye Teşkilâtı: XVII. Yüzyılda Tersâne-i Âmire.* Ankara: TTK, 1992.

Bostan, İdris: "Tersâne-i Âmire", *Türkiye Diyanet Vakfı İslâm Ansiklopedisi.* 40, Istanbul 2011, pp. 513–516.

Börekçi, Günhan: *Factions and Favorites at the Courts of Sultan Ahmed I (r. 1603–17) and his Immediate Predecessors.* Unpublished PhD thesis, The Ohio State University, 2010.

Burke, Peter: "The Invention of Leisure in Early Modern Europe", *Past & Present* 146 (1995), pp. 136–150.

Burke, Peter: "Reply", *Past & Present* 156 (1997), pp. 192–197.

Çağman, Filiz– Zeren Tanındı: *Topkapı Sarayı Museum Islamic Miniature Painting.* Istanbul: Tercüman, 1979.

Dalsar, Fahri: *Türk Sanayi ve Ticaret Tarihinde Bursa'da İpekçilik.* İstanbul: Sermet Matbaası, 1960.

Danişmend, İsmail Hâmi: *Osmanlı Devlet Erkânı.* [2]Istanbul: Türkiye Yayınevi, 1971.

Davis, Ralph: *Aleppo and Devonshire Square: English Traders in the Levant in the Eighteenth Century.* London etc.: Macmillan, 1967.

Değirmenci, Tülün: "Osmanlı Tasvir Sanatında Görselin "Okuması": İmgenin Ardındaki Hikâyeler (Şehir Oğlanları ve İstanbul'un Meşhur Kadınları)", *Osmanlı Araştırmaları/The Journal of Ottoman Studies* 45 (2015), pp. 25–55.

Değirmenci, Tülün: "Sözleri Dinlensin, Tasviri İzlensin: Tulû'î'nin *Paşanâme*'si ve 17. Yüzyıldan Eşkiya Hikâyeleri", *kebikeç* 33 (2012), pp. 127–147.

Denny, Walter: "Music and Musicians in Islamic Art", *Asian Music* 17/1 (1985), pp. 37–68.

Dilek, Kaan: "Şerefeddin Ali Yezdi", *Türkiye Diyanet Vakfı İslâm Ansiklopedisi.* 38, Istanbul 2010, pp. 550–552.

Eldem, Sedad Hakkı: *Köşkler ve Kasırlar.* I, Istanbul: Devlet Güzel Sanatlar Akademisi, 1969.

Erdoğan, Muzaffer: "Osmanlı Devrinde İstanbul Bahçeleri", *Vakıflar Dergisi* IV (1958), pp. 149–182.

Erdemir, Ayşegül Demirhan: "Emîr Çelebi", *Türkiye Diyanet Vakfı İslâm Ansiklopedisi.* 11, Istanbul 1995, pp. 129–130.

Eslami, Kambiz: "'Emād Hasanī, Mīr, 'Emād-al-Molk", *Encyclopaedia Iranica* VIII, Costa Mesa, CA, 1998, pp. 382–385. Digital version: http://www.iranicaonline.org/articles/emad-hasani-mir_

Eyice, Semavi: "Davud Paşa Sarayı", *Dünden Bugüne İstanbul Ansiklopedisi.* III. Istanbul: Kültür Bakanlığı/Tarih Vakfı, 1994, pp. 8–9.

Eyice, Semavi: "İbrahim Paşa Sarayı", *Türkiye Diyanet Vakfı İslâm Ansiklopedisi.* 21, Istanbul 2000, pp. 345–347.

Faroqhi, Suraiya: "Fireworks in Seventeenth-Century İstanbul", Arzu Öztürkmen – Evelyn Birge Vitz (eds.), *Medieval and Early Modern Performance in the Eastern Mediterranean.* Turnhout: Brepols, 2014, pp. 181–194.

Faroqhi, Suraiya: "Mohair Manufacture and Mohair Workshops in Seventeenth-Century Ankara", *Ord. Prof. Lütfi Barkan'a Armağan.* = *İstanbul Üniversitesi İktisat Fakültesi Mecmuası* 41/1–4 (1982–1983), pp. 211–236.

Faroqhi, Suraiya: "Ottoman Textiles in European Markets", Anna Contadini and Claire Norton (eds.), *The Renaissance and the Ottoman World.* Farnham, Surrey: Ashgate, 2013, pp. 231–244.

Gibb, E. J. W.: *A History of Ottoman Poetry.* (*HOP*) III, Edward G. Browne (ed.), [2]London: Luzac, 1965.

Göyünç, Nejat: "Eski Malatya'da Silâhdar Mustafa Paşa Hanı", *İstanbul Üniversitesi Edebiyat Fakültesi Tarih Enstitüsü Dergisi* I (1970), pp. 63–92.

Göyünç, Nejat: "Silâhdar Mustafa Paşa Hanı'na Âit Bir Vesika", *İstanbul Üniversitesi Edebiyat Fakültesi Tarih Dergisi* XXV (1971), pp. 73–78.

Gündüz, Filiz: "Okmeydanı", *Türkiye Diyanet Vakfı İslâm Ansiklopedisi.* 33, Istanbul 2007, pp. 339–340.

Hammer, Joseph von: *Geschichte des osmanischen Reiches.* (*GOR*) V, Pest 1929, reprint: Graz: Akademische Druck- u. Verlagsanstalt, 1965.

Hann, Christopher M.: *Tea and the domestication of the Turkish State.* Huntingdon: Eothen Press, 1990.

İlgürel, Mücteba: "Kösem Sultan", *Türkiye Diyanet Vakfı İslâm Ansiklopedisi.* 26, Ankara 2002, pp. 273–275.

İnalcık, Halil: *Has-bağçede 'Ayş u Tarab: Nedimler, Şâirler, Mutribler.* Istanbul: İş Bankası, 2011.

İrepoğlu, Gül: *Imperial Ottoman Jewellery: reading history through jewellery.* Feyza Howell (trsl.), Istanbul: BKG, 2012.

Kaçar, Mücahit: "IV. Murâd Devrine Ait Manzum ve Minyatürlü bir Gazânâme: Tulûi'nin Paşanâme İsimli Eseri", *Türkiyat Mecmuası* 21 (2011), pp. 267–280.

Kafadar, Cemal: "How Dark is the History of the Night, How Black the Story of Coffee, How Bitter the Tale of Love: The Changing Measure of Leisure and Pleasure in Early Modern Istanbul", Arzu Öztürkmen – Evelyn Birge Vitz (eds.), *Medieval and Early Modern Performance in the Eastern Mediterranean.* Turnhout: Brepols, 2014, pp. 243–269.

Karatay, Fehmi Edhem: *Topkapı Sarayı Müzesi Kütüphanesi Türkçe Yazmalar Kataloğu.* II, İstanbul: Topkapı Sarayı Müzesi, 1961.

Kaya, Bayram Ali: "Yahyâ Efendi, Zekeriyyâzâde", *Türkiye Diyanet Vakfı İslâm Ansiklopedisi.* 43, İstanbul 2013, pp. 245–246.

Koçu, Reşad Ekrem: *Türk Giyim, Kuşam ve Süslenme Sözlüğü.* Ankara: Sümerbank, 1967.

Kreiser, Klaus – Christoph K. Neumann: *Kleine Geschichte der Türkei.* Stuttgart: Philipp Reclam jun., 2003.

Kut, Günay: "Acâibü'l-Mahlûkat", *Türkiye Diyanet Vakfı İslâm Ansiklopedisi.* I, Istanbul 1988, pp. 315–317.

Kuzucu, Kemalettin: "Tea as a New Flavour in the Ottoman Culinary Culture", Arif Bilgin – Özge Samancı (eds.), *Turkish Cuisine.* [2]Ankara: Republic of Turkey, Ministry of Culture and Tourism Publications, 2015, pp. 243–259.

Lentz, Thomas W.: – Glenn D. Lowry: *Timur and the Princely Vision: Persian Art and Culture in the Fifteenth Century.* (Exhibition Catalogue) Los Angeles: County Museum of Art, – Washington: Arthur M. Sackler Gallery, Smithsonian Institution Press, 1989.

Levend, Agâh Sırrı: *Türk Edebiyatında Şehr-engizler ve Şehr-engizlerde İstanbul.* Istanbul: Baha, 1958.

Marfany, Joan-Lluís: "Debate: The Invention of Leisure in Early Modern Europe", *Past & Present* 156 (1997), pp. 174–191.

Meienberger, Peter: *Johann Rudolf Schmid zum Schwarzenhorn als kaiserlicher Resident in Konstantinopel in den Jahren 1629–1643. Ein Beitrag zur Geschichte der diplomatischen Beziehungen zwischen Österreich und der Türkei in der ersten Hälfte des 17. Jahrhunderts.* Bern: Herbert Lang, – Frankfurt/M.: Peter Lang, 1973.

Meninski, Franciscus à Mesgnien: *Thesaurus Linguarum Orientalium Turcicae, Arabicae, Persicae: Praecipuas earum opes a Turcis peculiariter usurpatas continens nimirum lexicon Turcico-Arabico-Persicum ....& grammaticam Turcicam... etc.* Viennae 1680.

Meredith-Owens, Glyn Munro: "Ken'ān Pasha's expedition against the Cossacks", *British Museum Quarterly* XXIV (1961), pp. 76–82.

Mujezinović, Mehmed: *Islamska Epigrafika u Bosni i Hercegovini.* I. Sarajevo: Veselin Masleša, 1974.

Murphey, Rhoads: *Exploring Ottoman Sovereignty: Tradition, Image and Practice in the Ottoman Imperial Households, 1400–1800.* London-New York: Continuum, 2008.

Müller-Wiener, Wolfgang: "Zur Geschichte des Tersâne-i Âmire in Istanbul", Jean-Louis Bacqué-Grammont – Barbara Flemming – Macit Gökberk – İlber Ortaylı (eds.), *Türkische Miszellen: Robert Anhegger Festschrift, Armağanı, Mélanges.* Istanbul: Editions Divit Press, 1987, pp. 253–258 and 268–269.

Müller-Wiener, Wolfgang: "Das Kavak Sarayı – ein verlorenes Baudenkmal Istanbuls", *Istanbuler Mitteilungen* 38 (1988), pp. 363–376.

Necipoğlu, Gülru: *Architecture, Ceremonial, And Power: The Topkapı Palace in the fifteenth and sixteenth centuries.* New York: Architectural History Foundation; Cambridge, Mass. – London: The MIT Press, 1991.

Necipoğlu, Gülru: “The Suburban Landscape of Sixteenth-Century Istanbul as a Mirror of Classical Ottoman Garden Culture”, Attilio Petruccioli (ed.), *Gardens in the Time of the Great Muslim Empires: Theory and Design.* Leiden-New York-Köln, 1997, pp. 32–71.

Nutku, Özdemir: “Clowns at Ottoman Festivals”, Arzu Öztürkmen – Evelyn Birge Vitz (eds.), *Medieval and Early Modern Performance in the Eastern Mediterranean.* Turnhout: Brepols, 2014, pp. 195–202.

Ostapchuk, Victor: “Five Documents from the Topkapı Palace Archive on the Ottoman Defense of the Black Sea against the Cossacks (1639)”, Bernard Lewis – Omeljan Pritsak – Gönül Alpay Tekin – Şinasi Tekin – Gilles Veinstein (eds.), *Raiyyet Rüsûmu: Essays presented to Halil İnalcık on his Seventieth Birthday by his Colleagues and Students.* = *Journal of Turkish Studies* 11 (1987), pp. 49–104.

Özbilgen, Erol: “Eski Malatya’da Silâhdar Mustafa Paşa Hanı’nın Restitüsyonu Hakkında”, *İstanbul Üniversitesi Edebiyat Fakültesi Tarih Enstitüsü Dergisi* I (1970), pp. 93–102.

Özcan, Abdülkadir: “Güreş”, *Türkiye Diyanet Vakfı İslâm Ansiklopedisi.* 14, Istanbul 1996, pp. 317–320.

Özcan, Nuri: “Murad Ağa, Şeştârî”, *Türkiye Diyanet Vakfı İslâm Ansiklopedisi.* 32, Istanbul 2006, p. 185.

Özcan, Nuri: “Murad IV. Mûsiki”, *Türkiye Diyanet Vakfı İslâm Ansiklopedisi.* 31, Istanbul 2006, p. 183.

Öztürk, Mürsel: “Hâtifî”, *Türkiye Diyanet Vakfı İslâm Ansiklopedisi.* 16, Istanbul 1997, p. 468.

Pakalın, Mehmet Zeki: *Osmanlı Tarih Deyimleri ve Terimleri Sözlüğü.* I–III. [2]Istanbul: Millî Eğitim Basımevi, 1971.

Pamuk, Şevket: *İstanbul ve Diger Kentlerde 500 Yıllık Fiyatlar ve Ücretler, 1469–1998/500 Years of Prices and Wages in Istanbul and Other Cities.* Ankara: T.C. Başbakanlık Devlet İstatistik Enstitüsü, 2000.

Pekin, Ersu: “Evliya Çelebi’nin müzik kaynakları”, Hakan Karateke – Hatice Aynur (eds.), *Evliya Çelebi Seyahatnamesi’nin Yazılı Kaynakları.* Ankara: TTK, 2012, pp. 286–341.

Reindl-Kiel, Hedda: “Das Ende einer Kavaliersreise – Beginn einer osmanischen Karriere?”, eadem – Seyfi Kenan (eds.), *Deutsch-türkische*

Begegnungen/Alman Türk Tesadüfleri. Festschrift für Kemal Beydilli/Kemal Beydilli'ye Armağan. Berlin: EB-Verlag, 2013, pp. 106–187.

Reindl-Kiel, Hedda: "The Chickens of Paradise: Official Meals in the Ottoman Palace (Mid-17th Century)", Suraiya Faroqhi and Christoph Neumann (ed.), *Glorious Table, Prosperous Home: Studies in the Ottoman Material Culture of Food and Housing.* (= Beiruter Texte und Studien Bd. 73, Türkische Welten Bd. 4) Istanbul-Stuttgart: Franz Steiner, 2003, pp. 59–88.

Roemer, Hans R.: "Hosayn Bāyqarā", *Encyclopaedia Iranica* XII, New York, N.Y., 2004, pp. 508–5011. Digitalised version: http://www.iranicaonline.org/articles/hosayn-bayqara

Sahillioğlu, Halil: "Dördüncü Murad'ın Bağdat seferi menzilnamesi (Bağdat seferi harp jurnalı)", *Belgeler* II, sayı 3–4 (1965), pp. 1–36.

Sariyannis, Marinos: "Time, Work and Pleasure: A Preliminary Approach to Leisure in Ottoman Mentality", idem (ed.), New Trends in Ottoman Studies: Papers presented at the 20th CIÉPO Symposium, Rethymno, 27 June – 1 July 2012, pp. 797–811. E-publication: http://www.univie.ac.at/ciepo/wordpress/wp-content/uploads/2011/07/downloaded1.pdf.

Şenödeyici, Özer– Halil Sercan Koşik: "IV. Murat'ın Bağdat Seferi Hakkında Yazılmış bir Kaside: Tulû'î'nin Pesendîde-Nâme'si", *Akademik Sosyal Araştırmalar Dergisi* 2, sayı 2/1 (2014), pp. 133–150.

Stchoukine, Ivan: *La peinture turque d'apres les manuscrits illustrés. II, De Murad IV à Mustafa III, 1623–1773.* Paris: Geuthner, 1971.

Tanındı, Zeren: "A Treasury for Bibliophiles: Ottoman Illuminated Books", *Distant Neighbours, Close Memories: 600 Years of Turkish-Polish Relations.* (Exhibition catalogue: Sakıp Sabancı Museum) Istanbul: Sakıp Sabancı Museum, 2014, pp. 96–109, 117–119.

Tezcan, Hülya: *Atlaslar Atlası: Pamuklu, Yün ve İpek Kumaş Koleksiyonu/Cotton, Woolen and Silk Fabrics Collection.* Istanbul: YKY, 1993.

Tezcan, Hülya: "Furs and skins owned by the Sultans", Suraiya Faroqhi – Christoph K. Neumann (eds.), *Ottoman Costumes: From Textile to Identity.* Istanbul: Eren, 2004, pp. 63–79.

Titley, Norah: *Miniatures from Turkish Manuscripts: A Catalogue and Subject Index of Paintings in the British Library and the British Museum.* London: British Library, 1981.

Uluçay, M. Çağatay: *Padişahların Kadınları ve Kızları.* Ankara: TTK 1980.

Uzunçarşılı, İsmail Hakkı: *Osmanlı Devletinin Merkez ve Bahriye Teşkilâtı.* ²Ankara 1984.

Uzunçarşılı, İsmail Hakkı: *Osmanlı Devletinin Saray Teşkilâtı.* ²Ankara: TTK, 1984.

Uzunçarşılı, İsmail Hakkı: "Osmanlılar Zamanında Saraylarda Musiki Hayatı", *Belleten* XLI/161 (1977), pp. 79–114.

Yıldız, Murat: "Padişahların Dinlenme ve Eğlenme Mekânları: İstanbul Bahçeleri", Feridun M. Emecen, Ali Akyıldız, Emrah Safa Gürkan (eds.), *Osmanlı İstanbulu. (Uluslarası Osmanlı İstanbulu Sempozyumu II, 2014).* Istanbul: 29 Mayıs Universitesi – İstanbul Büyükşehir Belediyesi, 2014, vol. II, pp. 633–673.

Yılmaz, Hasan Kâmil: *Azîz Mahmûd Hüdâyî ve Celvetiyye Tarîkatı.* Istanbul: ERKAM, 1999.

Yılmaz, Hasan Kâmil: "Celvetiyye", *Türkiye Diyanet Vakfı İslâm Ansiklopedisi.* 7, Istanbul 1993, pp. 273–275.

Yılmazer, Ziya: "Murad IV", *Türkiye Diyanet Vakfı İslâm Ansiklopedisi.* 31, Istanbul 2006, pp. 177–183.

Zilfi, Madline: "Women and Society in the Tulip Era, 1718–1730", Amira El Azhari Sonbol (ed.), *Women, the Family and Divorce: Laws in Islamic History.* Syracuse, N.Y.: Syracuse University Press, 1996, pp. 290–303.

Zorlu, Tuncay: "Ottoman Ship Launching Ceremonies: A Practise between Symbols and Rites", *International Review of Turkology* I (2008), pp. 55–63.

For further titles see: www.ebverlag.de

Otto Spies Memorial Lecture
edd. Stephan Conermann & Gül Şen

Reihe: Bonner Islamstudien (BIS)
Herausgeber der Reihe: Stephan Conermann

Reihe: Bonner islamwissenschaftliche Hefte (BiH)
Herausgegeber der Reihe: Stephan Conermann

Reihe: Ulrich Haarmann Memorial Lecture
ed. by Stephan Conermann

Reihe: Narratio Aliena?
Herausgeber der Reihe: Stephan Conermann

ebv BERLIN

EBVERLAG DR. BRANDT WWW·EBVERLAG·DE

Rainer Kuhl
Jägerstraße 47
13595 Berlin

Tel.: 00 49 30 68 97 72 33
Fax: 00 49 30 91 60 77 74
E-Mail: post@ebverlag.de